THE
EXCHANGE STUDENT

HARPA AMIN

AuthorHouse™ UK
1663 Liberty Drive
Bloomington, IN 47403 USA
www.authorhouse.co.uk
UK TFN: 0800 0148641 (Toll Free inside the UK)
UK Local: 02036 956322 (+44 20 3695 6322 from outside the UK)

This book is printed on acid-free paper.

ISBN: 978-1-6655-8425-8 (sc)
ISBN: 978-1-6655-8426-5 (e)

Print information available on the last page.

Published by AuthorHouse 01/20/2021

authorHOUSE®

In loving memory of my
AFS brother Frank Webb.

Contents

1

The Adventure Begins

"Don't come back engaged," was a sentence many people said to me when they knew I was going to study in America.

I told them I would do no such thing. My dream had come true. I was also so lucky to be able to go to the state I most wanted to, California. One could not ask for any specific place.

The reason people said this to me was probably because many Icelandic girls had been involved with either British or American servicemen stationed in the country during the war and afterwards.

Some of them got married and settled down in the US or Britain. Others had children, which they had to take care of by themselves. Those soldiers left Iceland and were never heard of afterwards.

Iceland was a Danish colony until 1944. On May 10th, 1940, the British army invaded Iceland and took over the only radio station that was at that time and some official buildings. They were afraid that Iceland would be invaded by the German Nazis after they had invaded both Denmark and Norway.

I was born in down town Reykjavik. The French Embassy was very close by, and the American Embassy on the next street. I often saw the American airmen. They would give the children chewing gum, which was not available in the shops. I also got some.

There were a few cinemas, and I used to see all the films I wanted to. Most of them were American shown a few years after their release in the United States. Snow White and the Seven Dwarfs was a favorite and I saw it many times. Roy Rogers and his horse, Trigger was also very popular. Abott and Costello, Tarzan, Dean Martin and Jerry Lewis were regularly shown.

There were also some German and Scandinavian films shown. None of these films were dubbed nor had subtitles until much later. It was a film called 'I Confess.' And then I learned my first sentence in English, "I don´t know." I was very proud when I asked my playmates what this meant. They would say, "I don´t know," in Icelandic. And I would say, "That is correct." From an early age, I dreamt about one day going to the United States and meeting some of those actors. I even wrote a letter to Elvis Presley. And I saw all his films.

Later, I moved to a suburb which was like living in a small town in the countryside. It was nice growing up there, but the dream about America was not forgotten. One day I saw an opportunity.

I had recently read an interview in the national newspaper with two young men who had just returned after having been exchange students in the US. I thought this was something I wanted to apply for. So I did. I had to send all kinds of references, my score at school, (lucky, I had been with the highest in my class the year before and my name appeared in the newspaper) essays and so on. It might have helped that I had also been abroad before and travelled to The Faroe Islands, Norway, Sweden, and Denmark.

One day in February the postman delivered a letter to me.

I was really thrilled to open it and read it. I was so overwhelmed with excitement that I wanted to jump with joy. I had been selected to become an exchange student with The American Field Service and would go to the United States.

I was getting a scholarship in a high school, free schoolbooks, medical bills (not for the dentist) and all trips within the country. I was to stay with a family as one of their members.

I would pay for my travel to and from Iceland to New York and bring pocket money and of course, my clothes and other personal items.

I was alone at home and wanted so much to tell somebody the good news. So I went to my next door neighbour and did that.

My hard work had paid off. There was a lot of preparation to be done in the next coming months. I had neglected my dentist, so I had to make a few visits there. I even had to have some teeth pulled. I had to be in the best of health to participate. There was a demand for a blood test and an X-ray. I had to show this X-ray at the border.

In the next months, we would get more information from our local AFS office. And we met up with former AFS students who told us all about their experiences. We were invited to parties, and also to the American Library, where American AFS students who were staying in Iceland, told us some more and sang American songs. There was a slideshow with photos from different parts of the USA.

A farewell party was held for us where only English was spoken, plus we got a Coca Cola in a tin. We found that rather funny because we had never seen soda before like that, only in glass bottles.

I was busy during the summer working in a fish factory to earn as much money as possible for my America trip. In Iceland, it is customary for students to earn money during the summer. Some also have a part time job during the winter. I had been earning some money from the age of seven. First, by walking with babies in a pram in my neighbourhood. Then I sold newspapers in the downtown area. Later I did more babysitting, worked on farms, in a biscuit factory, but most of my summers I worked in some fishing factory because there was a better chance there to make more money.

Sometimes we would work until eleven in the evening. There was a bus that picked us up and dropped us. This bus did not go all the way to my home. I had to walk about fifteen minutes. I used these minutes to practice thinking in English. I had learned Danish from the age of twelve. That was the first foreign language we learned, then English, and in the last two years of high school I also learned German.

During the summer, I got letters from my American family, the Janiches. They lived in Long Beach, south of Los Angeles. Nick was the father, who worked for the Los Angeles authorities.

Willie worked in a kindergarten, and their two daughters, Millie and Carol were the teenagers in the family. It was compulsory in this program to have children of similar ages as the exchange student to be able to participate. They sent me photos of the family, and the house, and their Buick. In one photograph Millie was all dressed up in a formal gown to go to the prom with her boyfriend. This was all very exciting. I also wrote back to them and told them about my life in Iceland.

I bought them an Icelandic sheep skin, and I also bought records with Icelandic artist to be able to play for them and others.

My grandmother had given me a new suitcase. And I had to repack because I had packed far too many things. I had to take my typewriter with me. I had been visiting friends and others came to see me, too, before leaving.

Many friends came to Reykjavik airport to see me off and wish me all the best. It was not every day that teenagers were traveling to the other side of the world, and staying for a long time. Some friends had given me presents, among them a little doll dressed in a nice Icelandic costume. The flight was not until in the evening, so I went in the afternoon and had my hair done. I had to look nice for this very first flight in my life. I had gone on a ship to the Scandinavian countries two years before. My mother baked the traditional Icelandic pancakes for us, with jam and whipped cream. All set to go with Loftleidir Icelandic to New York.

We were twenty-one Icelandic exchange students from different parts of Iceland who went together.

I got a seat at the very front of the plane and sat with a boy called Oddur who lived in Akureyri the main town in the north of Iceland. I found it exciting to be on that plane. And I could not sleep. This was a long flight. We landed in Goose Bay, in Labrador, Canada.

We were allowed to get off the plane for a while. After flying in darkness for hours it got brighter, and we could see many cities below. We flew over Long Island and Manhattan and could see the skyscrapers. I saw that many people seemed to have swimming pools near their houses. Finally we landed at Idlewild airport, which was later named after John F. Kennedy and in short called JFK airport. I was feeling a little sick after the flight. This trip had taken twelve hours.

When we went through the customs, and I was afraid I would have to pay customs for the sheepskin, but that did not happen. The director of AFS, Mr. Stephen Gallatti and others were waiting for us at the airport to greet us. Our health certificates were examined. We were divided into a few taxis and off we went to different locations in the city. Some stayed at an AFS accommodation and some at The Commodore hotel which advertised that it was the best located hotel in New York.

I stayed there with two Icelandic girls, Sigridur Gunnarsdottir, and Anna Ingolfsdottir on the sixteenth floor. We could see skyscrapers all around and that was a bit overwhelming. I thought New York was amazing and not like anything else I had ever seen.

We got a very nice room with a television, radio, telephone, and of course, there was a bathroom. The lobby was huge, with beautiful carpets. Under the building was a mall full of shops. We would have our

HARPA AMIN

meals at the AFS dormitory at 313, East 43rd Street. It took us more than an hour to find it the first day. The same evening we were invited to go to the Empire State Building' which was the tallest building in the world.

A young black boy wearing shorts came and walked ahead of the group through the streets of New York. There were many signs that read 'Walk' or 'Don´t Walk.' I had never seen this kind of signs before. There were so many people waiting at each sign that once, I was almost pushed into the street in front of a car. Lucky, I managed to stay on the footpath. Otherwise this adventure would have ended right there. Too bad it was raining, so the view from the Empire State Building was not as good as we had hoped for. We got some tickets allowing us to come back later because of this.

The next day we visited the United Nations on the banks of the river Hudson. We did not understand everything thee guide was telling us because this girl was talking very fast, and like a robot. She was trying to tell us everything there was to know about this remarkable institution. We saw many of the meeting rooms and so on. Afterwards I and another Icelandic girl, called Inga Sigurdardottir from The Westman Islands, went on our own to look for the biggest shop in the world called Macy´s. It was with departments on five floors, and lots of things to see. In the evening there were entertainments at our hotel. Spanish exchange students showed us Flamenco.

Our short stay in New York was over, and time to get back to the airport. The exchange students were spread all over the states. I went with American Airlines, which was full of students from around the world. Anna Ingolfsdottir and Erla Thorarinsdottir were among them. I sat next to a boy from Belgium, and a girl from Germany. I felt the United States was big because it took five hours to fly across to the west coast, and I got a bit airsick on the way .My American family was at the Los Angeles airport waiting for me with a sign that said 'HARPA-POLY-JANICH.' I was supposed to go to a school, which was called Long Beach Polytechnic High School, always called Poly High. After a few photos had been taken, we headed to my new home in Long Beach.

We drove on the highways and freeways and through some loops. That was an experience. We had no such things in Iceland. The Janich family lived at Daisy Avenue. It was as the name says an avenue with two streets in the opposite directions and beautiful trees in the middle. The house was a brown timber house, similar to houses I had often seen in movies. We walked right into the living room through a door, which also had mosquito blinds. There was a fire place, a sofa and a television. A dining table was at the end, where there was another room, which the parents used as a bedroom. There was a shower in that room, and a sliding door into the patio and garden. There were banana trees and flowers, and a nice swimming pool with a dive board and stairs. There were two other bedrooms. Millie had one, and Carol and I shared the other one. There were walk in wardrobes as is customary in this country and a bathroom in the hall. There was also another door where one would go directly into the kitchen. The laundry room was at the end of that. Behind the house was a garage, and from there an alley leading to the streets. The family had a dog called Queenie which was eleven years old. She was nice looking, white and brown.

I was not used to having a dog in my family but she was good and made no trouble at all.

2

New Life In A New City

It was of course beautiful sunshine next morning when I woke up in the new environment. I had unpacked and put my clothes in the walk in wardrobe (the closet).

I put a big photo of my Icelandic boyfriend Jonas on the cabinet beside my bed. It was a nice photo of him with a short haircut looking a bit like an American. I had only known him a few months before I left, and we had not promised each other anything, so this was not serious.

We were going to correspond with each other. There were many other people who expected to hear from me, and my new experience. I started writing letters and the postbox was just on the next corner, so it was easy for me to put my letters there.

I was excited to use the swimming pool. I knew how to swim and liked that but I was not good at diving. I practiced and practiced diving from the diving board, but never became any good. Many other young people came there every day. John Jolliffe was one of them .He came the first morning. He was tall, with very short hair, handsome with a nice suntan. I thought he looked like a native Indian. I later found out that he was adopted, and was really from Hawaii. I liked him a lot. His parents were related to Willie.

A few girls came by one day to practice some dance steps, and used also pompoms. They had been chosen in the spring to be Song and Flag girls at the school. They were practicing dances that they would perform at the football games .I was surprised because in my country we had a total holiday from school during the summer, and did not need to think of it at all. We were working every summer, and only had a short break right before the school started.

We went to Poly High, and I could choose my subjects. English, American history and Physical Education were compulsory so there were not many to choose, since the same subjects were every day. I chose German and French. I also had to take Public Speaking, since I was to make speeches about Iceland wherever there was an opportunity in the next months to come.

The school did not start until in the middle of September, so there was an opportunity to go places, and meet new people and practice my English. Some people were surprised that I could communicate a bit. Most people did not know much about Iceland, nor that Icelandic is spoken there. Since I have always been very talkative I was hoping to be able to speak English fluently real soon.

I was very excited to watch the black and white television. We did not have one in my home. I saw a program about Miss International shortly after arrival. The famous actor Lorne Green from Bonanza was hosting this, and Miss Iceland, Gudrun Bjarnadottir was among the contestants.

We went to a baseball game the night after with some members of the family, and a friend called Vivien. I had never seen this kind of a game. It was similar to a game we used to play in the streets at home, hitting a ball with a stick, and then running in different corners. We would call it corner ball after those corners, and I guess it is similar to cricket. Then all of a sudden Vivien said "She won, she won!" And I asked "who won?" "Miss Iceland, she won the Miss International competition," she replied. I could not believe my own ears. But it was true. I had followed all beauty competitions in Iceland and cut out the photos of the contestants from papers and magazines, and of course also of Gudrun. This was a great accomplishment for her and would be in media all over the world.

I was invited for a formal dinner party in her honour. The Icelandic ambassador was there too. Pictures of Gudrun and me were taken. I have never seen those photos, but an article came in the national newspaper in Iceland where it was mentioned that I, the exchange student, had attended. I was surprised to see Gudrun because I saw that her hair was auburn. It had always looked like she was a brunette in black and white photos. She was a very modest and interesting girl, with a lot of charm. Some film studios had made a seven years contract with her, but she was not at all interested in such things, and did not go through with that. I was sitting next to an Icelandic actor. His name was Petur Rognvaldsson but he called himself Peter Ronson in a film where he played an Icelander in the first 'The Journey to the Center of the Earth' film, based on the story by Jules Verne.

He was working in Hollywood on some other film projects. Carol was also invited with me and to many other events. She was a junior in my school where I was a senior, and that is probably why this was, and not Mille who turned eighteen, and was getting ready for college. She also had a boyfriend by the name of Larry.

I was invited to a trip in an MG convertible car and Carol came with me. We spent the whole day going to different places, among them to a newspaper. I got my name written on a metal piece, like is used for printing.

The girl who drove us told us that she had changed her last name. I did not understand how people could do this, just like that. I have had to spend a lot of hours explaining our name system, which is very different from most other countries. You may have noticed that all the Icelandic girls I have mentioned have a last name ending in 'dottir'. I was Harpa Josefsdottir because my father was Josef Sigurdsson, and I was his daughter (dottir). Had I been a boy I would have been Josefsson (son of Josef). My mother was Adalheidur Helgadottir the daughter of Helgi. Women did not change their last name when they got married. How could a woman be named Sigurdsson? She could never be the son of anybody, least of all her father in law! Later the law changed, and children could have a last name where they were either the son or daughter of their mother and even both parents. Our last names are not family names, so we never refer to them as such. On the other hand there are a few family names, which are from the time of colonialism when Icelanders changed their names so they looked more Danish. I used to say, when explaining the name system, that in case I would marry a foreigner, I might be able to add his last name. I guess I knew deep inside I would do this. On the other hand I was not legally able to do this until the law changed. Then I had been married to my foreign husband for thirty years. We always use our first names and don´t address people with Mr., Mrs. and so on. Only the president is addressed in such a way (if people remember!) and sometimes the bishop.

We had gone for a drive in August and saw Christmas lights in the streets. I found this very odd, and got the explanation that the people in that area were able to choose which one they wanted to have at Christmas time.

I went shopping and bought a pair of trainers, which they called tennis shoes. Willie gave me a dress which was called mumu and was from Hawaii. Even though I had brought some summer dresses I did not have the same kind of clothes girls wore in California. Most of my dresses were sewn by my mother. They were nice, unique and other girls would not have the same. There were a lot of adjustments to the new family, culture and climate. There was sunshine every day, as expected. But one night there was heavy rain, thunders and lightning and people woke up. It had not rained in September for about a hundred years. I just slept like a log, and did not hear anything. I sure did not miss the rain in Iceland.

The food was very different. In my home we would usually eat different kinds of fish five days a week and twice meat dishes. In those days fish was much cheaper than meat. The meat was mainly lamb, either fresh, salted or smoked, and either cooked on a pan, or in an oven. We also had meatballs and fish balls. We never ate vegetarian food and very seldom salad with the food. We had potatoes, peas and carrots. Chicken was a luxury. We had different kind of deserts, soups, puddings, trifles etc. Before my parents bought a refrigerator, my mother used to make ice cream in our garden, when there was snow. She used harsh salt and snow to make it. Here we were eating spaghetti, tacos, potato salad, some steaks, chicken and barbeque. The last thing was something I had never even heard of before. Apart from bacon, I had never eaten pork. Even the water was different. To me water was just water that we could drink from the tap. I had never heard that there was soft or hard water. Here it was hard. Ours is soft so we never have to use salt in machines to make it soft.

We went to many potluck parties, which was also new to me. Most of you know that it is when a group of people bring all kinds of food to a table, and everybody can take what they like to eat, and have fun together. I learned a new word in my first one and that was sink. Somebody told me to put something in the sink, when I was helping in the kitchen. I liked the potato salad and made my own recipe that I am now going to share with you.

Potato salad.

One kg. potatoes(about 2lbs)
One onion
On red paprika (bell pepper)
Two tomatoes
One teaspoon salt

1/2 a teaspoon freshly ground pepper
Two tablespoons mayonnaise
One tablespoon crème fresh
One tablespoon ketchup
One teaspoon mustard

Method: Boil the potatoes and cool them. Peel and cut them into small pieces. Cut all the vegetables into small pieces. Put the spices, ketchup, mustard, mayonnaise and crème fresh on top of the potatoes and mix very well. If you have a left over you can keep it for a few days in a refrigerator.

Bon appetite!

Of course I kept on learning more words and phrases. One was saying "Thanks a lot" when somebody was teasing me or making fun of me. I learned that it was called commercials the advertisement, that kept on coming on the TV.

I watched the television when Martin Luther King junior. marched with about three hundred thousand people in Washington DC for more civil rights for his people. Many whites were there too. It was impressive to see all these people who believed it would lead to better life. He said the unforgettable sentence "We shall overcome". This was all in the hope that things would improve for black people. People sang this song and it became a slogan and people would sing this for the next many years to come.

There was an Icelandic-American society in Southern-California. I was invited to a dance which was held in Inglewood. I got an interesting and nice dress to wear. It was black and white and reminded me of some southern bells.

I met many Icelanders who lived in the area. Among them was a girl named Eyglo Antonsdottir and we became friends. She had come to visit her aunt, who had moved there with her husband and a child. They had wanted a new life in sunny California. Eyglo had actually got papers to emigrate from Iceland to the US, and had been working, and later worked as an au pair for some families. We went to the dance, and among others I danced with a man named Philip. He was a lot older than I. He wanted to know what I was doing in the evenings. He wanted to see me again. I said I was always studying, because I did not want to meet up with him again.

We stayed overnight at the home of a lady, who had married an American serviceman. Her name was Hulda Dunbar, and she had grown up children. One was going to a military school. The next day we were roaming around in a park in Inglewood.

My family took me to Knottsberry Farm, which was an interesting amusement park. All of a sudden I heard somebody calling my name. How would they know this, or know something about where I came from? The family had arranged this for fun. We had some posters printed. One of me as a dancing girl in a saloon, and one of my friend Jonas as a wanted person. I was going to give it to him later.

I went with a group of youngsters to Disneyland in Anaheim, and some of the foster mothers were driving. Suphan, John, Carol and many more were there. We saw a lot of interesting things, and got on many rides and that was a lot of fun. We were also able to dance. John asked me to dance and I said

I did not know how to. He was good in driving electric bump cars. He also had his own car a yellow Volkswagen Beatle.

The first time I went with my family to the popular restaurant called Hof´s Hut, they told me that there was a famous actor there. He was called Walter Brennan and was currently playing in a show on TV called 'Beverly Hillbillies'. I had never seen this, nor heard anything about the actor. They all urged me to go and ask for his autograph, which I did. It was the first one of many others that I collected during the year.

I went to see Summer Holiday with Cliff Richards and The Shadows and really enjoyed the film and all the songs. New to me was that there was also another film shown at the same time. It was The Nutty Professor with Jerry Lewis. When we arrived at the theater it was in the middle of that movie.

I did not have to do any housework apart from keeping the room clean, and once in a while do the dishes. There was a strange brush we used for that. There was no dishwasher. I also had to take the PE outfit home on Fridays and have it was washed. Then I had to iron it. Willie told me I should hold the top by the collar. I guess I was not ironing the way she did. When I iron shirts, I have thought of her ever since .Nick was rather quiet and often relaxed by the pool.

One day Willie came home in a sort of a shock. She had been in a store shopping, and a man came inside with a gun and robbed the shop. Fortunately nothing happened to her. This was America where many people had guns. This was like it was in a movie. This is also why so many people other countries are scared and just don´t want ever go to the United States.

I had to attend many meetings with other AFS students. We would compare notes, and talk about how everything was going. We got a booklet where I read that we were supposed to ask the foster parents if we could call them mom and dad. One day I asked my foster mother whether I could call her mom. She said: "Just call me Willie". It came as a big surprise. I felt then that she did not really want me to be a part of this family as one of her daughters. I felt I was just like all the other kids who came there every day to swim.

One day I had to be of assistance at my AFS club at school. We were talking to kids who had applied and wanted to become exchange students. This was after school was finished, so I came home a bit late. Willie got very, very angry with me for coming so late. I had no idea in advance that I would be late home, and there was no payphone that I could use to let her know. I was devastated by her reaction. At home I was an independent person and a taxpayer. I was the eldest of my sisters and a role model. I was used to my parents totally trusting me. Here I felt often I was being treated like a little kid. I was not allowed to go further than to the mailbox on the corner by myself. I hid myself in our closet. I could hear them calling and looking for me. They found me there crying. I felt really miserable.

Carol and I were dropped at the school in the morning and always walked the same streets on the way back after school. If Carol was not there for one reason or another I would walk totally different streets to see something new. I understand that they were trying to protect me and were also responsible for me. I felt this was like I was being very restricted. Carol always sat in the front seat, and I in the back.

Vivian took me for a ride to Hollywood. It was very nice of her to do this. We saw the Chinese Theater, Hollywood Boulevard and the stars on the pavement there. I found this fascinating and saw the names of many of the actors I knew from seeing their films back home.

Before the school started I spent a lot of time in or around the swimming pool. We sometimes played 'Ping Pong' which I had not seen before. It was fun, even though I was not very good.

Most days John was with me and others in the swimming pool. He flirted a lot with me. I think Carol had a crush on him, and she did not like this at all. Willie was very strict, and I don´t think she would ever have allowed Carol to date anybody this much older. I also talked about my boyfriend and made him think that I only thought about my boyfriend back home, even though I liked John a lot. He could also see that the letters from him came pouring in. One day he drove me in his little VW beetle and invited me to his house. He showed me his room. He had a closet full of nice clothes and lots of beautiful things. He was the only child, so it looked like he got everything he desired.

One day I went with Millie and other girls to the airport to welcome a football team back from a game in another city. Her boyfriend Larry was one of them. This was called a homecoming. Everyone was very emotional. I didn´t understand why.

3

Long Beach Polytechnic High School

My school, called Poly High was an old and a very respectable high school. It was established in 1895 and it was the home of scholars and champions.

I was to study here different subjects and graduate with a High School Diploma in the spring which I did and will tell you more about that later. One was able to learn all sorts of things according to your interests and after graduation one could either apply for going to college or a university all depending on your grades. The school was divided into three semesters and at the end of each we would get a card with our grades. We had to take this home and let the parents or guardians sign the card to acknowledge that they had seen it. Then we had to take the cards back to school, and show the teachers.

There were around 3.600 students attending the year I was there. The school campus had many buildings, some with school rooms, offices, a library, a cafeteria, a restaurant, shops, a big auditorium, sports arenas and a swimming pool and gardens. Behind the school was a huge area for attending all sort of sports. Many famous athletes have studied here and some played with famous American football teams. Others participated in the Olympic Games like my friend, Martha Watson.

There was a very powerful music department, and all kinds of bands, a brass band, symphonic orchestra, a dance band, and a Big Band. The school has received many Grammy prices. There were four choirs and a country group. People could study everything about dancing, drama, acting, staging, journalism and printing to name some. One of famous people who studied at Poly High were none other than the actor John Wayne, and also Spike Lee actor and a musician. Much later were actress Cameron Diaz and Snoop Dog, actor and a musician. There are probably more that I don´t know about.

The emblem of the school and a lucky animal was the rabbit, and the colours of the school were golden and green. We were called Jackrabbits. All kinds of rewards were given for good achievements. A gold L, an L with one diamond or two diamonds. Many boys wore yellow and green jackets with a big L on them.

After spending a whole month in California my first school day arrived. I had been to a lot of places and had met a number of people and had been able to practice my English. Now it was serious business. Every school day started with the flag raising ceremony in the middle of campus, both the American flag and a California flag. Boys who had the intention to join the military forces did all kinds of ceremonies there. They belonged to the so called ROTC and got all kinds of training regarding the military. They also wore special uniforms similar to army uniforms.

In the first period everybody swore a legend to the nation and country, and put their hand on their heart. I just stood there and listened respectfully. I was not an American. I learned German and the teacher was Mr. Frankenbach, American history with Mr. Schaber, French with Mrs. Harway, English with Mrs. Hopper, public speaking with Mr. Ross and physical education with Miss Kellogg. We had the same subjects every day, and would have to go between the different classrooms. We had a locker, where we could keeps our books between classes, since it was not customary to have the books in school bags. Sometimes we would go to a special language lab where we would sit with headphones and listen to the pronunciation of the languages we were learning.

In English I learned of course a lot of new words. Also learned what the nouns and verbs were called in English. I had to write some essays too. One of them was about teaching somebody how to tie laces.

Some of the buildings were called bungalows, and Mr. Schaber had his classroom there. He was considered to be the strictest teacher of them all. The kids that were with me in this history class were a year younger than I because the ones my age had finished this course, and were now studying humanities subjects. When it got really hot once, we had to go with the lessons into the auditorium because it was cooler there. We were supposed to take an exam from our notes. The trouble was that

I had not written a single note, and was just like a stupid. I had just listen the best I could. After that I was very active writing down notes, and typed them on my typewriter and handed them in. We got grades for this also. I wrote an essay about many interesting things in history, among them about the attack on Pearl Harbor on December seventh 1941. The bungalow was old, and the chair I sat on was not good, so I got once a thick splinter in my finger. I took it out, and the school nurse, that I had to go to, was very impressed that I had done this myself.

In Public Speaking we had panels discussing all kinds of things, like the dating custom, marrying early(by the way if a girl fell pregnant or married she had to leave school), common courtesy, how to place plates and cutlery on a table for parties, and many more. We had to make short speeches about different subjects, like phobias, 'God helps those who help themselves' and ' When there is a will, there is a way,' and more. I liked the last idea a lot. This was all helpful, when I started to give speeches in different kind of clubs and schools. We had to write down some notes on cards to remind us of what we were going to talk about. We did not have written speeches.

John Jolliffe was with me in this class. Mr. Ross recorded us when we made a short talk, and introduced ourselves. In the English class I told the students about Iceland.

The students came from all levels of society. I found it interesting to see that some black girls colored their hair red. They also made their hair straight. I was not used to seeing black people at all, because they did not exist in Iceland at this time. They were also called coloured. There were many kids from Mexico and Hawaii. Some looked like they were from Japan. None of my schoolmates seemed to be natives .The boiling pot of cultures was there for sure. All the schools aimed for giving the best education whether you were going to be a worker, a doctor or a lawyer or anything else. The coffee brown Robin was with me in English and History. She was very nice. Susan Wentworth was with me in French, Public Speaking and in Student Government (another semester). She was also nice, and we often had lunch together to start with when I hardly knew anybody. We could eat in a cafeteria, but I chose to eat in the good weather sitting on a bench outside somewhere. I got a sandwich with a lettuce and ham and sometimes a bag of potato chips with me from home. I got five cents to buy milk to drink with the sandwich.

Ron Jackobson was with me in French. He became a good friend of mine. We got to know each other, when I was trying to open my locker, and had no clue how to do this and he helped me. My locker was situated in front of the class room, where those lessons were. One had to use a secret number, and move the lock back and front like on a bank vault. We enjoyed writing notes to each other in French, during the lessons. We later kept on corresponding with each other for many years afterward, but not in French this time. Mrs. Harvey had almost moved to Iceland once and was supposed to stay at the army base in Keflavik airport. Everything was packed, and she and her husband were ready to go. On the last minute the plans changed, and they never went. She really enjoyed telling me this story.

Physical Education was always in the last period, and because the climate was so good we were most of the time outside. We played all kinds of ball sports, like basketball, volley ball, hockey and mini golf. The boys played American football, water polo, and all kinds of other sports, like swimming, sprinting, throwing balls, and so on. I was dressed in a uniform like all the other girls wearing blue shorts and a blue blouse. We had lockers there too for those clothes and towels. We started each day standing in rows, doing so called jumping jack exercises to heat up. Funny as it is, I became the leader of the basketball team, even though I had hardly any experience in that field. We sometimes played mini golf.

We were only inside if it was raining. I was good in many of the exercises because I had had a very good teacher at home. Part of our education in P.E. was also a sexual education and about drugs. I will never forget a film we were shown about a girl who was trying to get off drugs. She was in horrible pain and her body was wriggling like a worm.

When I was introduced to some girls and they were told that I came from Iceland they would say "REALLY!" I guess they had no idea what kind of people lived there. I often had to tell people that we did not live in igloos, and that we were not Eskimos. Some Icelanders had fun telling Americans that we do and that we use elevators to go between the stories. Some people even think we are in one of their states. People have also been asked if they had taken the train. Of course there were many that I met and got to know, that were genuinely interested to know all kinds of things about Iceland, and Icelandic culture.

I noticed how happy people were, and they said "How are you?" I thought they wanted to know how I was. But very often they just did not have time to wait for the answer, so I soon learned that this was just a greeting. I think people were this happy because of the climate. At least they did not worry about it, and always talk about how bad it was, like is customary in my country, as well as in England. I was also happy about all the sunshine, and did not miss neither rain nor snow. To me it was amazing how many of the kids wore glasses, and had braces on their teeth.

Every Friday there was a meeting at the auditorium mainly to cheer the sport teams. The song and flag girls danced on the stage, and the cheerleaders called out phrases all to encourage our teams, whether it was the football, basketball or other sports. We were all singing too. On Friday evenings there was a football game. The player I noticed the most was of course John, and he had number eighty four on his outfit.

After the game, most of us went to the sports area where we would dance to records. The kids were standing in a row in a circle and danced. It was similar to country dances. John asked me to dance. I said no again to him because I did not know these dances .I knew how to dance jive, twist, rock and some old dances, but these dances were different. I noticed that girls were not shy to approach boys, and really let them know, if they liked them. I was not used to this kind of behaviour. It was called that they were fresh. In my culture the boy always had to take the first step, like asking a girl to dance.

The most popular song there was 'Louie, Louie.' I did not pay much attention to that there were almost only white kids there. The coloured kids had another place near the school. I never went there.

There were all kinds of announcements for events coming up. Sometimes there was something educational or entertainments. A man called John Goddele had travelled to eighty four countries. He came and told us about his travels in South-America. He had met Hal and Halla Linker, the Icelandic lady who had married an American after only knowing him for a very short time. They travelled the world, and made lots of television programs about their adventures for many years. Halla later wrote a few books about this too. The first one was called An Icelandic Adventure Bride. I met her once in Iceland, when she signed her autograph for me on one of her books.

I stood on the stage at the auditorium twice talking about Iceland and Icelandic culture. There were 1800 students listening each time on The AFS day at my school. I told them among other things about our oldest parliament in the world dating from the year nine hundred and thirty. Also about how Icelandic teenagers have fun and go camping in the summer time without their parents. The other exchange students who attended other schools in Long Beach also came, and talked about their countries. I was always wearing one of our national costumes, when I made speeches in different places. Bernard Kulla from Germany wore his special, short leather pants, Dida Neirotti from Italy wore an Italian dress, Naoto Kira from Japan wore a kimono and Aruna Taribagil from India wore a sari. She was often with me when we were changing into our costumes. She wore saris in different colours and shades. Never could I have imagined that I would ever wear one like that, leave alone that I would have plenty of them, and other types of Indian costumes. Once when I had invited the other exchange students for dinner, the girls were discussing whether they should buy some material, and have a sari. Not sure if they ever did. As many will know a sari is about seven meters of material, and it is wrapped around the body in certain ways. One also has to wear a petticoat underneath, and usually a tailored made blouse, plus you have to know how to wrap the sari. I had no interest at this time. Now I know this very well. I have also taught other ladies to do this. Of course I had no idea I would marry an Indian.

There were all kinds of clubs at the school for Latin, Spanish, German, Esperanto, French, mathematics, chess, cooking, future teachers, a flower group, art show group and a radio group that learned to make radio programs. We could also join The Red Cross, Kiwanis. AFS club and all kinds of girls and boys clubs by the names of Tabek, Rota, Portia, Caprice, Junior Exchange Chamber of Commerce, Senior Men´s Council, Girls League,Boys League, The Ushers Club and the Lettermen Club. Then there were kids who assisted at the cafeteria, or the library.

Of course I was in the AFS club and also in The American Red Cross, Portia club and Girls League, where I was the foreign representative. I was presented in the last one to all the teachers and made a small speech, and told them about Iceland. Most meetings in these clubs were early in the morning before school started. I had to sell some kind of shares in AFS for imbursement of the activities. I also sold programs for the football games.

Poly High issued a school paper, called High Life that came out every two weeks. It would report about activities on campus, and very much about achievements in sports, and lots of photos of those who had done well. Those who were interested in journalism worked there, and also those interested in photography. There was an interview with me and Suphan in the fall. Pictures were taken of us pretending to be eating hot dogs and drinking Coca Cola. Everything was a fake. We got no hot dogs nor Cokes. This was to show how we had become accustomed to American ways.

There was a photo taken of us under a world globe at the library, and this one appeared in The Press Telegram with an interview. Pictures came of us also in local newspapers. All seniors had a photo taken in the fall in a graduation outfit. This photo was then used in the yearbook in the spring. I used on of me smiling, but it was not a good one.

At all events and sports the song and flag girls played a big part. They were dressed in blouses with short sleeves, and a very short dress over it. On the front of it was the letter L. Polyettes were younger girls, who used pompoms and did all sort of stunts with them. They wore very similar outfits as the song and flag girls. The cheerleaders were all boys, and they wore long pants and jackets with an L on it and a bugle on the front. They would use big bugles when they sang and shouted. The big lucky charm animal, the rabbit, was called Jonathan. It was always there, and it was a girl called Sally, who was inside the costume. The brass band always played and the so called majorettes were in front of it. They were very impressive throwing their sticks in the air and catching them and all sort of other things. All this made a special atmosphere and we were all very excited to cheer our teams so they would win the games, and they very often did.

4

Phi Gamma Chi

Susan Wentworth introduced me in a meeting in a club, which was for girls attending Poly High. It was called Phi Gamma Chi .The club did on the other hand not belong to the clubs at the school. It was common that the names of such clubs were written in Greek letters, as this one was. I was interested in joining this club, even though I felt it was a bit of a snob club. All the most prominent girls and the popular ones belonged to it. I was proud when I received a letter, where I was formally invited to join as honourary member. I was officially sworn in the club in a solemn ceremony. I had to kneel on a pillow, put my hand on a bible, and swear an oath at a candle light. I got a necklace with the name of the club in Greek. Boys from a club called Kappa Sigma Chi had been invited to attend this.

It was difficult for the other girls to be able to be accepted into the club. I had the privilege of being the exchange student, and think that is why I was invited. The younger girls who wanted to become members had to pledge for it, and do all sorts of things. They almost became our slaves. We could ask them to do different things for us. Sometimes this got out of hand and the girls were desperate. In some way they were humiliated in a similar way new students are treated in colleges in Iceland at the beginning of their first year. Not all of the girls made it into the club. When this all was going on food was made in different places. We ate the appetizer in one home, went to the next one and ate spaghetti there and ended with a tart in the third house.

Every meeting started with the prayer Our Father, and I was glad to learn this in English. It was really nice to participate in all the events in this club, and the girls very also very nice to me. The club had a

Christmas Dance. I wanted to invite John to this dance, but Millie had already invited him. I went with the president of the Student Body, and his name was Norman Wilky. I got a very nice pink dress that my elder AFS sister Nancy had had before. She lived on the east coast. The dress was altered for me and made shorter, and some pleads were made in the skirt. It was customary for a boy, who picked up a girl to go for a date, to bring her a beautiful orchid to put on her arm or on the dress. Of course Norman gave me such a flower and put it on my arm.

Sometimes we had meetings where boys clubs were invited as was when I was sworn in. Those clubs were the same type as ours. I went to an Italian restaurant with girls in my club. After that we were all invited to spend the night at the home of my friend Louise Sully. This was called a slumber party like a pajama party. There was a trampoline there which we jumped and played on. I had never seen one like that and tried it for the first time.

When I had my eighteenth birthday the girls gave me a surprise party. We had all met at a playground and all of a sudden they appeared with a birthday cake for me and it said 'HAPPY BIRTHDAY' on it. This was totally unexpected. I also got a sweater with the name of our club and many birthday cards. This was so sweet of them.

Later I got a jug like a beer jug, and on it said HARPA HONORARY MEMBER. This was indeed a great honour. I still have it.

5

Activites

The AFS Long Beach was always organizing some activities for us. They had collected seven hundred dollars per student and they must have spent that money on all of this for us.

Pomona Fair.

Suphan and I got a free pass from school to be able to attend the Pomona Fair. It was a festival, where people displayed all kinds of crops, vegetables, fruits, cakes, all from the near farms and towns. They also had some other activities there. Suphan´s foster mother drove us. On the way the car broke down. It was going to take an hour to repair so we started walking along with Naoto from Japan and his AFS foster sister Barbara. On the way a police car drove up to us, and the officer asked what we were up to. We were of course supposed to be at school at this time. The officer offered to drive us to the fair grounds, and he did.

There was an international house. Since there was no Icelandic department so I was put with Tahiti! Just another island! There was a native Indian in full costume. He showed me some horses and gave me a postcard with a photo of himself, and wrote his autograph on it. I have always wanted to be on an Indian reservation, but have never been on one up to now.

We had lunch at a restaurant upon a hill in the park. All the exchange students were introduced, and it was announced where we came from. After that there was a dance, and it was a very nice day, even though it rained a little.

Universal City.

We were invited to visit Universal City which was a film studio and not open to the public like Universal Studios, which was later opened as an amusement park. We got to see all kinds of stages that were used in TV programs. We went into a large area where they were shooting a popular western program. The sky was painted on a big canvas, and there was mud on the floor. Everything was done to make it look natural, so the viewers would not realize that this was all taken inside a studio. There were many wagons like the pioneers used when crossing the United States on their way to the west. We were also shown how all kinds of things that are used in films, were made. We saw also where they were shooting an Alfred Hitchcock film called 'Three wives'. We ate in the same cafeteria as the all the actors and crew. We did not see anybody famous, except we got a glimpse of Gregory Peck for a minute.

Interesting things and places.

We went to South Gate and visited the General Motors car factory. We saw how cars were assembled slowly, slowly which was very interesting.

We went regularly for concerts where the Long Beach City Symphony Orchestra played on Sunday evenings. Sometimes there were famous musicians playing there. I got some autographs from them.

We were invited to an ice hockey game. Coming from Iceland, I still had never seen a game like that before. I knew how to skate, and we would skate on the pond downtown Reykjavik or on some frozen lakes near the city. All the AFS students were introduced and an Icelandic girl came to me and talked to me. I never saw her again.

We visited a home for the blind and were told about their way of life. We got to know something about The Braille alphabet also. I got a card with my name in Braille letters.

On New Year´s day there is a big parade in Pasadena called the Rose Parade. We were invited to go there. I invited Carlos from Chile with me. There were countless beautifully decorated floats, mostly with roses, but also other flowers. All kinds of other decorations were there in many different forms. There were actors who played in popular TV shows and they were dressed in the same costumes in scenes from these programs. Beautiful girls were dressed in beautiful dresses, but some of them wearing very little. This was all very impressive and nice to watch. Afterwards we went to lunch, and met up with exchange students from The Filipino Islands, Guam, Italy, Hong Kong and Kambodscha (now called Cambodia).

We were invited to see the Procter and Gamble soap factories. We were shown everything regarding making soaps. There was a slide show about the establishment, and we took a tour of the factory after that. This was very interesting. We got a farewell gift, a box with three Ivory soaps, a toothpaste and a toothbrush.

We visited a radio station called KLON which was at City College. We sat on a panel, and answered questions, and it was all recorded. We got to see slides about the activities of the college.

There was a swimming pool party at the home where Suphan stayed. His AFS brother was at the time an exchange student in Germany. I corresponded with his mother for many years.

6

Michael

I met Michael, called Mike first at the church. There was a Sunday evening program for the youngsters. He showed me the basketball hall, which he was responsible for. We danced together, and records were played. I showed the kids how we danced in Iceland. I first saw a popular drink called Root Beer. It was not a beer though and I tasted it. I would not have tried it if it had been beer since I never drink anything with alcohol in it. I found the taste very strange and did not like it. I preferred to drink Pepsi Cola or Coca Cola.

Every Sunday morning I went with the family to the church for a mass, and afterwards to a Sunday school. This was an Episcopalian Church and at every mass, money was collected for the church and activities. The government does not support any religions, and they are very many all over the country. I found this strange, coming from a country, where the majority of the population was Christian Protestant, and all churches were owned by the state. Only one Catholic Church is there, and a few minor religious groups. I also found it strange at my age to go to a Sunday school. As a child I had participated in all sort of religious activities in church, YMCA, Salvation Army and a group called Betania, which was close to my home The last one told us about the heathens in Africa, and sent missionaries to a place called Konso. I really wanted to go there one day. We got nice Bible pictures, which I collected.

After often dancing with Mike on Sunday evenings, we started to meet each other at the lunch break at school. He was nice, and sometimes bought me a Coke, chocolate or ice cream. He once bought an ice cream sandwich. I had never seen this before. Because I didn´t know, nor understand the dating system in the United States, there was a bit of a misunderstanding between us. We had our lunch together, but he was also seeing another girl, who was with him in the brass band, and played a flute. That´s why I called her the Flute girl. Of course he could be with any girl he liked, and it was none of my business.

I thought this was strange, especially because he kept on saying how much he liked me, and told others too. What I was used to was that a boy was only with one girl at a time. Here it was totally different. Boys would ask different girls out, and if they asked the same girl out many times, they decided that now they would go steady, as they called it. I was not interested enough in Mike to be going steady with him, even though we also kept on dancing with each other at those church dances. The kids at school asked me who this boyfriend of mine was, and I always said there was nothing like that going on between us. He had told me that he was scheming on me, and I did not understand what that meant. Then some girls came and said to me "you are the girl Mike likes. " "Do you like him"?

One day I felt it was time to make things clear between us. I really did not mind if he would choose to be with the Flute girl rather than me, so I told him this. So I guess he chose her. We stopped hanging out together. Mike´s sister Pam was a good friend of mine and we often ate lunch together. Of course I would see Mike once in a while after this somewhere like at football games or other activities at school. He graduated with me in the spring. I was actually much more interested in John. But even though he often flirted with me, he was always meeting another girl called Sally, and I often saw them together on campus.

7

The American Field Service

When I applied to become an exchange student, I certainly didn´t know much about this organization. Neither what it was about, nor what it stood for. Of course I later learned about all of this, and why it all started, and also why it became an exchange program for young people at the age of sixteen to eighteen years old.

There were American servicemen during the First World War who volunteered as ambulance drivers in France. This corps was officially created by A. Piatt Andrew on April 15th 1915.They repeated this in the Second World War and then the leader was Stephen Galatti who was now serving as the president of AFS. After the war in 1946 he established The American Field Service International Scholarships with the intention of inviting students from abroad to study in the United States. The first students who participated came from ten countries: Czechosolovakia, Estonia, France, Great Britain, Greece, Hungary, The Netherlands, New Zealand, Norway and Syria and they were there during the 1947-1948 school year. The students had to be nominated by their teachers.

That is how AFS was transformed from a war time humanitarian aid organization to a secondary school exchange, volunteer and intercultural learning vision. It was to build a more peaceful world by promoting understanding among cultures. The name changed also later to AFS Intercultural Programs and it is non-governmental, non-profit. It provides these intercultural learning opportunities to help people develop the knowledge, skills and understanding needed to create a more just and peaceful world. A global citizen what this is also all about. AFS expanded and in 1970 it became multinational and students from the US traveled far and wide, and later other students also went to countries all over the world, and to all continents. Later there was also a program for teachers who could go to different parts of the world.

There was one very strict rule. We were not allowed to drive any vehicles, and not fly with private planes. If anybody did this they were sent back home immediately. I did not have to worry about this because I did not have a drivers´ license yet.

There was a motto which I really liked: 'Walk together, talk together, all ye people of the earth and then and only then will ye have peace'. I have tried to live by that motto ever since. I love meeting people of different cultures and backgrounds, and I can even communicate with them without a common language. I had to do this when we became volunteers for the Red Cross, when refugees from Viet Nam came to stay in Iceland. We were a foster family for them. They did not speak any English and we did not speak Vietnamese. Somehow we managed.

Some years after I returned to Iceland our AFS chapter was just about to give up. We could not send any students to the US and sent for the first time students to Europe instead. Then I became a volunteer for AFS, and served on different committees. I was a PR person and a counselor for almost thirty years. I was a counselor for a boy from Sri Lanka, who came from Italy, a girl from Canada, a girl from Ghana, a boy from Turkey, a girl from Belgium, a girl from Thailand, a girl from Germany and a girl from China. My family hosted some exchange students for a few days (I am not mentioning them here), short programs and the year program. The ones who stayed with us were: Doris Irizarry, a Puerto Rican girl, who lived in New York, Sabin Imhazzly from Switzerland, who now lives in New Zealand, Mark Barnum from Newport Beach, California, now in Seattle and Yuyun Feng from Shanghai, China (lives now in Melbourne, Australia). We have visited all of them and some of the others, and some of them have visited us too. This friendship is for life. I have also always been I touch with my own AFS families.

I will forever be thankful to AFS for this opportunity to meet all these different people and also all the nice friendships. It most certainly opened new horizons for me.

8

A New Home

I was very busy putting some curlers in my hair one evening. I was also watching TV at the same time.

I did not have too much to study that day. All of a sudden ladies from the AFS chapter appeared, and told me that AFS in New York had decided that I should move from the Janich family to another family. I would be happier there. A letter had also been sent to my parents from AFS New York informing them about this change. They were really worried about me. All this totally caught me off guard. Even though I had been telling about how things were in this home, I never even thought other than just staying there for the rest of the year. I would be there, no matter what. I am not a quitter at all. Nobody had mentioned this possibility before neither at the AFS meetings, nor in the family. I was to move the very next day, so there was not much time to pack, and get ready to go. Millie helped me to pack. This was not easy. I didn´t know much about what kind of a family I was moving to.

I was driven to the Webb family who lived at the other end of town to California Avenue in Knoxby Hills. I felt that I was being transferred from one jail to another, but of course it was not really like that. The family was the mother Margaret, called Peg, the father E. Ray, always called Ray and his mother.

They had four children: Nancy was the eldest. She was already married, and had moved to North-Carolina (I never met her), Reed who was studying law, married to Mary Ann an elementary school teacher, and they lived somewhere else and the twins Frank and Marge fourteen years old, who were still at home.

Then there was the grandmother, mother of Ray living in a little house in the garden. Ray was the vice president of Texaco oil and Peg stay at home mother. She did not have to do much housework because her mother in law did most of the cooking in the evening. We also went very often out to eat in restaurants. Sometimes it was a Mexican one, and that was something very new to me. In my home there was never spicy food. My mother only used curry when she cooked lamb, and made a bechamel sauce and put curry in it.

There was a Polish woman who came twice a week to do the chores. She cleaned and ironed the clothes. She changed all the beds every week. Peg really liked to play bridge and she did that with some lady friends in the afternoons. The grandmother was also interested in bridge.

Suphan lived close by and so did one of my school sisters Kathy Nesbitt and Louise Sully.

When we arrived at the door I could hear Frank inside in front of the door and the dog Ferdinand jumped and jumped. He was not less excited to see who was coming. Ferdinand was a very nice dog, black and white.

The house was very nice on two floors. On the ground floor was a hall with a guest WC, a den where there were books, and a huge collection of National Geographic magazines, and a television set, (shortly after I moved in DAD bought a color TV), living room where there was a sofa set and a piano, another living and dining room, a kitchen, and a room where Frank stayed and he had his private bathroom with a shower. There was a garage which was not used for cars because Frank had a huge train set there, and he kept on adding some features and tunnels to it. It was fun to watch this when the trains went full speed up and down hills and through tunnels.

From the dining room was a sliding door into the garden, where there were lemon trees. Marge often made lemonade for us from those lemons. She also taught me how to eat and appreciate celery with peanut butter on it. I have also taught my grandchildren to eat this. Peanut butter and jelly sandwiches were also very popular. We also had often bread with garlic. It was roasted in the oven. At first I felt that was a strange taste but got used to it.

Marge and I had our own rooms upstairs with our closets but shared a bathroom. Peg and Ray had a beautiful bedroom there too with a closet on one side and an en suit next to it with a shower. My room was a good size with a bed and another one underneath and that one could be taken out. My girlfriend Eyglo sometimes stayed over and used that bed. There was a good desk and a chair. I had a special board on the wall where I could stick all kinds of things I collected. Some were souvenirs. I had got a scrapbook, and started to put things in there too. This was the first time I ever had a room of my own because our house at home was so small that there was only one bedroom, where my parents slept with my four year old sister. I and my sister who was eleven slept on a sleeping sofa in the living room.

I really liked the new family, and all the surroundings. I had much more freedom. It was too far to walk to my school, so I got a lift with my school sisters, who lived in the neighbourhood. They either drove themselves or their mothers took turn in driving us. Teenagers in California could get their drivers licenses at the age of sixteen, and most of my friends had passed this exam and some even had a car of their own. In Iceland we had to be seven teen years old to get our license and in most cases teenagers could not afford to buy a car of their own and had to borrow from their parents.

Sometimes I had to walk a distance to take a bus to school, but never used the yellow school bus. Long Beach had a lot of oil, and on the way to and from school I watched a lot of oil pumps. I got now fifty cents a day to buy some food for lunch. If I did not spend it all, I saved some and kept in a shoebox in my closet. I also saved some of a fourteen dollar check I got as pocket money every month sent from AFS. I didn´t know if that was some money I had already sent them before. In the spring I managed to buy a nice suit. Eygló and I had gone shopping and wore our outfits to a fashion show shortly before she returned to Iceland. She was not interested in staying in California any longer.

I soon started calling Peg MOM and Ray DAD. Some years before, they had hosted another exchange student. It was a boy from Argentina. I found out later that I was only meant to be with them temporarily, but they applied to keep me in their home. A short time before they had been to an AFS event, where they watched me making a speech in my Icelandic costume, and talk about Iceland. I was really fortunate.

Halloween.

I went to two Halloween parties. One was at the home where Cathy from France was staying. We went on a scavenger hunt, and we had to go from house to house and ask for all kinds of things that we had been asked to find, and also look for them in the area. I had never done this before, and enjoyed it. I had also never heard about Halloween before nor All Saints Day, except in some stories I read as a child.

The same evening I moved in with the Webb family Suphan and I went to another Halloween party at the home of Kathy Nesbitt. We were both wearing black scary costumes with skeletons on, and were unrecognizable. Earlier in the evening I had also worn this, and gone with Frank from house to house begging for sweets by saying "Trick or Treat" like all kids did. The parents were there ready with full bowls of all kinds of sweets for us and others in the neighbourhood. The custom was that if they did not want to give us anything we were supposed to do some trick to the people. This was totally new to me and perhaps I was a little bit too old for this but I had fun anyway.

Suphan and I had to take a strange route and climb over fences to be able to arrive at the house where the party was. We went inside through an open window. There were many kids there, and nobody recognized us. Then they started talking about us and wondering why we had not arrived yet. I was laughing and laughing. I had trouble not making one of my school sisters grab my mask, and take it off. She was really excited to know who was behind this mask. Kathy Nesbitt had called my home to find out whether we were coming or not, and was really surprised when she saw us. By that time we had already been there for about forty five minutes. This was funny. After this we went on another scavenger hunt, and this time we had to drive around to find the things. Suphan went home early to do some studies.

9

Kennedy

Jim Musgrove came rushing into the French lesson at Mrs. Harvey. "He is dead" he screamed very emotional. We were all in a shock. What in the world was happening? Some students had been talking about it at the break that two to three shot had been fired at John F. Kennedy, the president of the United States where he was on an official visit in Dallas, Texas. But we could hardly believe this. We had asked Mrs. Harvey if she knew if this was true, and she confirmed it. Jim told us that many people had been watching television in some classroom, and everything was revealed. Kennedy was my favorite president, and I was supposed to meet him at the end of stay at the White House in Washington DC. I had followed his presidential campaign and was very happy when he won Richard Nixon in 1960. Now was November 22nd 1963.

There was no more teaching for the rest of the day. Everyone was in a shock. We went over to the classroom, where the television was, hoping to see something, but were told to go to the auditorium. All students and teachers were gathered there. It was a Friday, and it was customary anyway to gather there to cheer our football team, and announce about other activities on campus. This evening was the main game of the year The Homecoming Game because the Friday before it had been postponed due to rain.

The Principal asked everyone to stand up and be silent for thirty seconds in respect of Kennedy. We girls were crying. The band started playing happy songs, just like nothing had happened. I really felt sorry for the kids who had to dance, and also shout some cheerful songs. It must have been very difficult.

When I came home all radio- and television stations had news about the assassination, and I watched what I could. In the evening I went to see this special Homecoming football game, where my school was playing against a team from Santa Ana. Before it started the girls who had been chosen to be princesses were driven into the field in convertible cars. They sat on top of the cars wearing beautiful white dresses, and had on white high heeled shoes. Their hair had been done in a fine fashion.

I got permission from some boy who had a field pass to go there so I could take photos of them. Otherwise it was forbidden to go there.

This was not a normal beauty competition, more like competing who was most popular in the school. I knew all the girls because they were in Phi Gamma Chi, my club. One of the girls, Bonnie Cheeseborogh was chosen to be the Homecoming queen, and sat down in a high chair on a platform. After she was crowned she put her hands in front of her face, and seemed to be totally surprised. Still all this had been announced at the school before. The boys who had driven the cars stood side by side with their princesses. Their names were Susan Wentworth, Dena Macrate, Marcia Merritt and Carol Fraenkel.

Before the game began there was a silence for a short time in respect of Kennedy, after the national anthem had been played. We won the game 20/7.

In the next many days I was glued to the new colour television watching all the news about John F. Kennedy. I watched when he and his wife Jacqueline called Jackie drove in a fancy open car through the streets of Dallas. There was sunshine and beautiful weather. The whole event was shown again and again. The shots went off and another man Governor John Conally was also hit, but not fatally. He and his wife were in the front seat of the same car Jackie and Kennedy were in. Jackie held his head and her beautiful pink clothes were all bloodstained. Nobody knew at that time what was happening. Lots of security guards were all around, all in vain. Nobody could stop the killer.

After it was clear that Kennedy was not going to survive this attack, the vice president Lyndon B. Johnson was called upon. It was also shown when he took his oath as the new president of the United States of America aboard Air Force one, the presidential jet. Jackie was still wearing her bloody clothes. What a horrible ordeal! Mr. Johnson and his wife Lady Bird had also been in the convoy, but much further down the road, and nothing happened to them.

Very soon Lee Harvey Oswald was arrested suspected of having murdered the president. It was believed that he had been in a deserted warehouse in the neighbourhood, and just waited there for the chance to shoot and kill the president. He had been working in this six story high building, and it was easy to watch all the cars passing by. To this day it has not fully been proven that he actually did this all by himself, or perhaps there were some others who conspired. At least he was in this building, and when policeman J.D.Tippit wanted to question him, Mr. Tippitt was shot to death with a revolver. A hidden rifle was found at the site but not sure who owned that one.

Oswald always denied killing Kennedy and Tippitt as well. Were there other people there nearby? The Warren commission used years and years to investigate these murders, and nothing was to be revealed until after many, many years. It was said that many witnesses had disappeared, and were never to be seen again. This case became more and more mysterious.

According to information on the internet it did not come clear until 2007, when a man called Gary E. Marlow died. He had been the one who shot Tippit.

Lee Harvey Oswald had been living in the Soviet Union for a while and had a Russian wife and two children. He had wanted to give up his American citizenship and become a Soviet citizen, but this did not happen. It was said that he had both connections with FBI and KGB, but it was not confirmed. All kinds of ideas and thoughts were on this subject in the media for a long time.

It never came to that Lee Harvey was condemned for neither of those murders, even though he was accused the next day. When he was being transferred to a prison on November 24th all of a sudden a man named Jack Ruby appeared from the crowd and shot him in the stomach. Lee Harvey died of his injuries. This happened so suddenly that nobody was able to stop Ruby, even though there were lots of people around. There were cameras rolling all around from different television stations so this murder was alive, the first one in the history of the United States. Again the public was totally stunned. Lee Harvey had recently turned twenty four.

Mr. Ruby was an owner of a nightclub and a petty criminal. He had worked for Al Capone in Chicago, and said he was doing a revenge for Jackie, the widow of Kennedy. Now there was no lack of witnesses and Ruby was arrested right away. He later commented that Lyndon B. Johnson had behind the murder of Kennedy, because he was the only one who gained anything from it. Ruby was sentenced to the death penalty. This sentence was altered and new trials began. They were never finished because he died of cancer before he could be sentenced again.

On the day of the funeral of John F .Kennedy there was no school, and we could watch it directly on TV. The whole thing was very solemn and dramatic. Jackie was dressed in black, and with a black wail. She had a lot of dignity about her. By her sides were her two children, Caroline six years old and John jr. who just turned three on the very same day. The casket was covered with the American flag, and was placed on a wagon that white horses pulled through the streets. When the wagon went passed the widow and her children, the little boy who was always called John-John put his hand to his forehead as a soldier in respect of his father. This was very remarkable, and the public was astonished and impressed by this.

The funeral services were at St. Mathews Cathedral, and Kennedy was buried in the Arlington churchyard in Washington DC. Around a million people were watching the ceremonies on the footpaths. Most of the dignities around the world attended, among them Prince Philip (husband of queen Elisabeth) of England, the prime minister of England Douglas-Home, Charles de Gaulle, prime minister of France, Haile Selassie, emperor of Ethiopia, Akhito crown prince from Japan. Martin Luther King was there too.

The same day and at the same time the funeral of Lee Harvey Oswald took place. Another time of this day J.D. Tippit was also buried. In the evening we went to a memorial services at our church in memory of J.F. Kennedy.

The whole world was in sorrow over what had happened to the president and many said they would always remember where they had been, when they got the news about this horrible event. Again and again his famous words were quoted: "My countrymen, ask not what your country can do for you, but ask what you can do for your country." It was also popular when he had been on an official trip in Berlin, Germany, and said to the public: "Ich bin ein Berliner", meaning I am from Berlin, and the people cheered him very much. American embassies around the world had books where people could write their names in respect in remembrance of John F .Kennedy.

10

Family Life

My new family belonged to the same kind of church as the Janiches the Episcopalian one.

It was the St. Thomas church we attended and I had wanted to go to before, but nobody was able to drive me there. I did not attend a Sunday school there nor did we go as early in the morning to church. After the mass DAD very often bought a bunch of doughnuts, which we all enjoyed. The whole atmosphere in this home was much more relaxed.

I kept a good relation with the Janich family the whole time, and visited them once in a while. They were nice with me and gave me a Christmas present, a birthday present, and also a going away present. They later moved from Long Beach to Stanton where they lived in a house where you could have animals behind their house. The area was with a security system and gates. My husband and I visited them once there and also met Millie and her husband and Carol. Some years after that they had moved to Lake Havasu City, and had a very nice house with a swimming pool, near a golf course. We visited Carol and Willie there after Nick had passed away.

DAD often had to go away on a business trip to France. Because I was learning French, we often chatted in that language at the dinner table. That was very useful for me. Later he divorced MOM, moved to France, and married a French woman much younger than MOM. He had two sons with his second wife. They lived both in Paris, and in a beautiful house in southern France. Frank who later learned to be an architect spent a year helping with enlarging the family home of his stepmother. It was a very successful transformation. I visited the new Webb family and their two sons twice with my own family.

I sometimes went to visit my girlfriend Eyglo, who had first been living in Compton. Once a Japanese woman asked us to come shopping with her in a navy base, and then invited us for dinner afterwards. Another time when I was visiting Eyglo, and we were shopping we met a Chinese man. He was eager to invite us for a drink. We went with him to a restaurant. He had just recently arrived from Hong Kong, and did not know anybody. He wanted also to invite us to Disneyland and Los Angeles, but we did not accept that, and never went with him.

Aida.

MOM invited me and Marge with her to see the opera Aida which the San Francisco Opera was staging in Los Angeles. Leontyne Price, a black opera singer sang the lead Aida. She was very good. I did not get to meet her. On the other hand Richard Chamberlain was in the audience. He was very popular on television, playing Dr. Kildare. I used to watch that program a lot. I met him and got his autograph on my theater program. He was much more handsome in real life than on the screen, I thought. He later played in many miniseries and The Thornbirds.

Thanksgiving.

I had free from school Thursday and Friday because of Thanksgiving which I did not know what was because it´s not celebrated in my country.

I went with the family and some other relatives to Elsinore which was a small village in the countryside with about two thousand inhabitants. Near to the village was a country house owned by the Texaco company, and the family could use. It was situated on a hill with a good view. There was a swimming pool and an orange tree. I was allowed to invite my friend Kathy Nesbitt with me. It had started to be a little cold both in the morning and at night time. I don´t know if it was the elevation or something else but my nose started bleeding twice. This had never happened to me before.

For the Thanksgiving dinner was a huge traditional turkey cooked for hours. I had never tasted this kind of food before. This was a nice and festive dinner party. We were enjoying this weekend, played badminton, went for walks and visited the Elsinore village. Somebody found a snake near the country house, and put it around my neck, and a picture was taken. It was certainly not a dangerous one, and not very big. I touched it, and it was the first time I had ever been near one. I was not scared at all.

On the Friday Kathy and I went with DAD, Reed and Mary Ann to Palm Springs. On the way there we stopped in the desert. We pretended to be lost and hungry, and had pictures of us taken there. There were beautiful flowers, and palm trees with dates. I picked up a few dates, and they tasted just horrible. I guess they were not ripe. For one reason or another I took a few of them, and brought back to our home. I wrapped them in foil, and put in a drawer. A couple of weeks later I found them there, and tasted them. They had gone ripe, and were delicious.

This weekend was a lot of fun.

THE EXCHANGE STUDENT

41

HARPA AMIN

THE EXCHANGE STUDENT   43

HARPA AMIN

THE EXCHANGE STUDENT 45

HARPA AMIN

THE EXCHANGE STUDENT

11

Christmas And New Year

I had bought many Christmas presents for my family in Iceland, and sent them early along with Christmas cards.

In this home a big Christmas tree was bought and set up in the living room, where there was the most height. The decorations from the years before were not used. This year they had chosen blue and silver colored decorations. The tree was decorated long before Christmas, not like we do on the 23rd of December. We don´t light it until at six o´clock on Christmas Eve. I had a black and white picture taken of me and had a Christmas card printed. I sent that card to all my friends and family in Iceland.

Before Christmas I went with MOM to see West Side story. I thought it was fantastic and loved all the songs. There was a piano in one of the living rooms. I sometimes tried to play something, but did not know very much. When I was a little girl I wanted to learn. We had no piano to use for practice and could not afford to buy one. When I was a fourteen I bought myself a typewriter instead! After all you have to use your fingers on that.

We went for a ride to look at Christmas decorations in Daisy Avenue. People had all kinds of Santa Clauses, reindeers and other decorations in front of their houses. Of course there was no snow, so it was not as much like Christmas. We also went with AFS students on a bus to Downey, and looked at Christmas decorations. Aruna from India and her family held a party. Near her home were canals, and all kinds of floats and boats with Christmas decorations were floating by. The canals went around two islands. This was impressive, and nice to see in the darkness. Marge came with me, and I also invited Carol.

Right before Christmas Marge and Frank were confirmed. There was a little party at home. Rather unlike what we are used to with a big party, and a flood of presents. Here were only the closest relatives. The weather was nice so the guests could be in the garden.

There was nothing special going on Christmas Eve, except that there was a dinner party. I decorated my room with some Christmas decorations. I had collected all my Christmas cards as I was used to from home, and did not open any as soon as they arrived, as was customary here. I got lots of cards, and many of them were with photos of the volcanic eruption at Surtsey in the fall. I opened them in the evening.

At midnight we all went to a mass. We had hung our Christmas stockings near the fireplace a few days before Christmas. A lady who was a friend of the family had handmade a big stocking for me out of filter with a nice pattern and decorations. I thought this was very nice of her. I had not even seen here before. I still have it, and every year I keep my Christmas card in it until I open them. I thought this was such an interesting custom, that I also made socks like this for my younger sisters, when I returned home. They were smaller, and not as nice as this one.

Christmas morning came and we were in our pajamas, and now we were allowed to have a look at the overfilled stockings. I got an incredible amount of things: A notebook with the notes for ´West Side Story', two colour films, two batteries for a radio I was using, a bookmark, a comb, a pen, a chalk, writing papers, a toothbrush and toothpaste, six pencils, air envelopes, a cap, seventeen dollars (because I was seventeen), a photo of DAD and the lady who gave me the stocking and lots of candy. I was really surprised about all this generosity.

We then opened our Christmas presents and I had never gotten as many presents before. I got: A photo album, four blouses, two nightdresses, a pen, six pairs of nylons, two purses, a pair of pants, a petty coat, an Icelandic song book, two dollars, a waistcoat, a table decoration, a photo, a record, knitted slippers, a bracelet, a needle cushion which was like turtle and a bath powder. Some of these presents came from my family and friends in Iceland. My girlfriend Erna sent me five packets of the Icelandic Opal, which is a very popular sweet, and not available here, and an Icelandic magazine.

After this we all went for breakfast at some friend´s house. We first had a grape fruit, which I found to be with a very bitter taste. All the kids then went for a swim in the family pool. There were guests for dinner at our house in the evening.

Boxing Day was not celebrated, and the Christmas tree was taken down before the New Year. I was used to having our tree until sixth of January, which is the last day of our thirteen days Christmas. That is why that day is called the thirteenth. Then we celebrate with bonfires and fireworks. We say farewell to all the Yule lads that have come to town, and now return to their parents in the caves in the mountains.

Reed and Mary Ann lived in Los Angeles, and we visited them right after Christmas. We visited a museum which was showing big skeletons of dinosaurs. That was very interesting. In the evening we went to an exciting basket ball game with the U.C.L.A team in The Los Angeles Arena. We stayed overnight, and the next day we visited the U.C.L.A. campus with lots of beautiful buildings.

Because of the time difference between Iceland and California (eight hours) my New Years Eve arrived earlier. I called my friend Eyglo, and wished her a Happy New Year. Then I sneaked into my closed and sang the song we always sing as we celebrate every New Year with. Mary Ann and Reed had a party at our house, and we played different games. I was allowed to invite Eyglo to the party, but she couldn´t make it, because some Icelandic friends came to pick her up. I was disappointed because I wanted to give her a necklace that I had bought for her for her birthday which was on January 1st.

There were no fireworks that evening at home nor anywhere else, and no bonfires. I found this a very strange New Years Eve. But the New Year came anyway.

After New Year I went with my family to San Diego. We were visiting their relatives, the Ericson family. Dave the son of the couple had been an exchange student in Denmark. We could therefore talk together in Danish for fun. Marge and I stayed at their home, but the others in a hotel. We could also use the swimming pool there. We played pool, which is like billiard. In the evenings we played a game called Tripoli, which is similar to Poker.

We went to a park which was with houses from many different countries. I had heard that Iceland was the third best country to live in, and mentioned this. Marge did not at all believe that this could be right. We started arguing about it, and I think that was the only time we ever did that. We always got along very well.

We also went to San Diego Zoo. The animals there were among the best collection in the world. Bears and elephants showed their skills and this was fun. It was a beautiful sunset near the Pacific Ocean, and we played there by running away when the sea flooded in. Frank ran into the sea, and said he was picking up shells for me. He was a bit attached to me. This was at the end of our Christmas vacation from school, which started in a few days again.

12

Daily Life

Everything evolved around going to school and doing my homework. I also had to participate in different activities both there and on the behalf of AFS, and other associations. A lot of time went for writing letters to friends and family. I still have all the letters I wrote to my parents. AFS gave me a pen pal to write to which was situated in New York, and we were in touch regularly. The letters came all the time from my friend Jonas. He was working hard at his school. But he also was making all kinds of plans for us in the future for some time. Then a different letter came from him. He had not been going to dances since I left, and then went to a dance. He had met a girl there, and they were going to get engaged. He said he was very sorry to do this to me. I guess he felt he was betraying me in some way. I told him this was all right he did not have to worry about me. After all we had not been engaged or anything anyway.

I had been easy getting used to my new family. I had many friends at school, mainly those who were with me in the PHI GAMMA CHI club. Those girls were very visible in all school activities. Louise Sully was one of them and lived near me and I often went together with her to school in the morning. We went together to see 'The Music Man'. Louise and I corresponded with me for many years. None of those girls became future friends. My Icelandic girlfriend Eyglo that I had met at the first Icelandic function stayed my friend and still is.

I went often to see films because I got a discount card from The Fox Pacific Theaters, and it was cheap. I also had a library card and a bus card. I got a fourteen dollar check sent every month from the AFS office in New York. I had to let this money last the whole month. It was all right because I am always thrifty, and did not use my money for anything stupid.

Somebody mentioned my neck, and thought it was not looking normal. Perhaps I had thyroid. I was sure I did not have this decease. MOM went with me to a doctor and a blood test was taken. Nothing was wrong with me, fortunately.

Our graduation photos were taken in the fall in advance. We were wearing grey gowns, but not the caps. Even though I did not like mine I had them enlarged to be able to send some home. This cost almost thirteen dollars, and DAD was so nice to me that he gave me ten dollars so I could pay for this. He went regularly on business trips to France and also on a six weeks trip to Africa in February. MOM had to go back East, as they called it because Nancy was going to have a baby. It was the first grandchild in the family.

Two Icelandic boys who lived in California came to visit me. They took me to a race course, where lots of races were held. We could some of those race cars.

All of a sudden I was bold! It was not like all of my hair had disappeared. No, it was a spot the size of a nickel on top of my head. I could comb my hair over it, so people could not see it. I have no idea why this happened, but think it may have been caused by the curlers I used to put in at night time, and kept in the hair overnight. I had to have my hair nice. I did not put permanent in my hair, as many of my school sisters did. Fortunately this has never happened to me again.

I sometimes got Icelandic newspapers sent from home among them some with lots of photographs from the volcanic eruption. I cut all of them out and kept them. I also saw picture of this in Life magazine and cut them out too. I have kept all programs and booklets, tickets, receipts, letters, memory book and of course my diary. All this has helped me recollecting all these memories, and how everything appeared to me. I also got an American newspaper sent to me for free.

When we were out driving we used to listen to the radio, and among the songs we heard were those of the Beatles like 'I wanna hold your hand', 'She loves you, yeah,yeah' and more. We would sing along those songs and enjoy them. The Beatles came to America and everything went crazy. These boys John Lennon, Paul McCartney, Ringo Starr and George Harrison were from Liverpool, England and had become so popular that now America wanted to see and hear them. They had much more hair than what was considered usual and people talked about this too. They appeared for the first time on The Ed Sullivan show which was a very popular show at that time on TV. We had to watch this, and hear all these nice songs like 'Till there was you', 'All my loving', Please,please me', ' I wanna hold your hand', and more. There were millions and millions of people watching this program. The majority of the people in the audience were teenage girls, who screamed and screamed.

13

The Trip To The Grand Canyon

Right before Easter Reed and Mary Ann took me and the twins to Grand Canyon. It was cold on the way, and had been snowing. Marge and Frank had never seen snow before. Reed stopped so they could play in the snow, and there were lots of snowballs thrown around. We drove to Flagstaff in Arizona and spent one night there. When we arrived at Grand Canyon we stayed at a hotel very close to the canyon. As the name includes it is an enormous canyon, and it was very impressive to see. There was snow over everything and very beautiful and totally magnificent. We could not see all the way to the bottom. It is possible to go down with donkeys, but that was not possible now. I would not have trusted myself to go down in this much snow anyway. The Colorado River has slowly, slowly dug this canyon. There is a national park there and one can see items that are many thousands of years old. Many different tribes have lived there, and still do. The Ericson family from San Diego was with us and we all had a lot of fun together. After a few days we continued our trip, and went to Las Vegas in Nevada. On the way we saw the famous Hoover Dam, which was huge and impressive. At least one hundred people lost their lives building it.

Big road signs were everywhere on the road leading to Las Vegas. Even though they were huge, they were nothing compared to the gigantic and different types of commercial lights in that city. Most of them were advertizing all kinds of clubs and hotels. We stayed at one of those fancy hotels. In the basement was a casino. The kids and I were too young to go inside. We just had a little peep. People had to be twenty one years old to be able to go inside, and do alls sort of gambling, and also insert money in machines.

Las Vegas is most famous for all those casinos and beautiful buildings, all built in the middle of a desert. I have never been there again, but know that many more fantastic buildings have been erected, many imitations of world famous buildings. I however went once to a place in Nevada, which was like a branch from Las Vegas, except a great deal smaller. Casinos are not allowed in all states. Indians have license to run them in many places.

On our way back home we visited a ghost town called Calico. Nobody lived there anymore. It looked a lot like towns that are shown in cowboy films. There had been silver and borax mines, and the town grew fast. When there was not much to gain anymore working in those mines, people just left, and everything was deserted. At a later time Mr. Walter Knott, the one who owned Knottsberry Farm in Buena Park, had bought the place, and turned it into a tourist attraction. We took photos where we could put our heads on the top of special statues, so we looked like cowboys. That was kind of funny.

14

School Life

We were not always just studying at school every day. There were all sorts of activities going on. Most of them were a lot of fun. When Mr. Schaber had a birthday my class celebrated it and there we did not have to turn in essays that day. Somebody appeared with a cake with the name 'Jimmy' on it. His name was James. Birthday presents were presented to him and all of them were nothing but jokes. He got a girdle with a saying: "Schaber´s retainer A-152", and there were balloons attached, like it was for a fat man. I had no idea what this A-152 meant. But to tell the truth Mr. Schaber was not a slim man, and only thirty four years old. This was all done just for fun, and he took it well.

Girl´s League had a tart competition between students and teachers. Only boys participated. Everyone had aprons on around their neck .Nobody was allowed to use their hands eating the tarts. The winner would get to throw a tart in the face of the one that lost. Ken Ludmerer lost, and tarts were thrown at him. He was totally covered, and his glasses were full of whipped cream. Everyone had fun at this event.

There was a water polo game between students and teachers. Again only boys played against male teachers. The boys were all wearing girl clothes. This was a lot of fun and so much commotion, that some that were not supposed to be in the pool landed there too.

Girls always had to wear a dress or a skirt. We were also supposed to wear different clothes every day. It was customary to wear matching colours and even shoes matching too. I got used t this and still like to wear matching clothes. I noticed that the girls were always making nice comments about how nice my clothes were. I was not sure if they really meant it every time. Perhaps they were just being polite or nice. Jeans or pants were forbidden. Except for one day when we were allowed to wear shorts or pants. This was a sports day and we had a trice race in the track field. I participated on the behalf of AFS, but Suphan did not turn up. The tricycles were not there on time either. They were old and stiff. I and had hardly started, when somebody had finished. I had thought it was a long race, but it was very short.

Hall of Fame was in the school and there were different kinds of trophies that students had earned. Frank Stirling was one of my school mates. He once showed me the Hall of Fame. There was a trophy there that he had earned for making speeches. He was very good speaker. He was interested in politics. He was in ROTC and planned on joining the air force later. I met him many times when some functions were held. Sometimes he drove me home, and we had nice conversations.

After Christmas I chose Drama with Mr. Johnson instead of my German class. I played different parts and also mimed with the music of West Side Story. Mr. Johnson was happy with my progress in English, and I got good grades there. I joined the Student Government instead of the Public Speaking class. Suphan had been there in the fall. There was a new government and now John Ingram was the president, after Norman Wilky. There was a formal dinner, and I had to make a speech. Afterwards we discussed the dating custom of young people. Susan Wentworth and I got the task to reorganize the school offices. In reality we hardly did anything but measure a lot, and make some sketches. At least nothing was done to change anything this spring.

I participated in the Spring Song. I was singing and dancing with huge colorful fans. We sang "Thank heavens for little girls." Maurice Chevalier had made this song famous. Then we sang a song from the musical ' Annie get your gun'. This was fun. I had been singing in some choirs in Iceland, and love singing. There was not time for me to add any choirs this time to my schedule, so I didn´t join any of them.

In the spring I went with the Student Government on a bus to Santa Barbara where we had a meeting. We were at a hotel by the sea, and could go to the beach. Suphan was located in a room with Gene Washington who was the only coloured student on the trip. I thought about why this was. Perhaps it was because Suphan also had a bit darker skin than the other students?? Gene was a very good scholar and also a good football player. He later became a professional player.

The girls played some tricks on the boys just for fun. We stayed only one night there. In the evening there was a dance, and we danced to records. Some became very romantic on the floor.

They were the ones who had been dating.

15

Always Plenty To Do

The local AFS chapter in Long Beach kept on organizing all kinds of cultural events for us. My family participated by inviting all the exchange students to the country house in Elsinore. Now that it was warmer it was possible to use the pool and some did that. I went with some of the students to the Elsinore Lake and swam there. In the fall the lake had been totally dry but one could see where it had been. I thought this was unusual for a lake to be there, and then disappear. We also went into the village for sightseeing.

Another day we were invited to an army hospital. There were injured soldiers. Some had lost their legs, and one could just see their stumps. I had of course not been to a hospital like this one before. We don´t even have any armed forces in my country. The police is not armed at all (only special squads). We had American armed forces stationed in Iceland for many years, and British before that.

We were invited to go to the CBS studios to watch a life Danny Kay show. The guest stars were Hayley Mills, and her father John Mills. I went afterwards and got their autographs. I thought it was the most fun to see Hayley, because she was my age, and very famous at this time. She had among others played in a film called 'Pollyanna' and a film about identical twins that traded places .The parents had divorced and one lived in the US and the other in England. Of course Hayley played both the parts. She got the honour of becoming the first teenager to get a star on the footpath on Hollywood Boulevard. Sidney Poitier who had been the first black actor to get an Oscar for acting in 'Lilies of the Fields' got his star around the similar time. I had gone to see this film, and was very impressed by his performances. I had seen ´Porgy and Bess' with an all black cast when I was 14. That was the first time that I felt a connection with black people. The AFS students in Long Beach and the one in Lakewood spent a lot of time together going to all these events.

We also went on the beach in Seal Beach together. It was nice weather and we enjoyed this. That was the first time I went on a beach in California, wearing a swimming costume. It is hardly ever warm enough in Iceland to do this.

As AFS students we were honoured by the mayor of Long Beach, and invited for a ceremony where we were given the key to Long Beach. I gathered that only very important and famous people used to get this and I know that beauty queens also got it.

On my 18th birthday Eyglo and I went to Disneyland. We enjoyed spending the day there.

We both had pictures drawn of us. I thought her picture looked more like her than mine did. My hair was too light and I did not even think it looked like me at all. I did not realize then that the sun had made my hair much lighter.

16

Othello

I felt that I was floating on a cloud in this fancy convertible car. I sat in the front seat, and Louise in the back. It was not because the car was new and very nice. It was some kind of a feeling I had never felt before. Terry was driving, and was going to take us to a coffee house, just like it was the most normal thing in the world. How he talked just lifted me onto some other plan.

I invited Louise Sully with me to a play. It was the tragedy Othello by William Shakespeare and it was shown in a student theatre in a college. I had invited Ken Ludmerer but he could not make it due to measles he got. I had to write a critic about this play for my drama class, and read it out loud. The play is like most people know about the Moor Othello, who was a general in Venis, Italy. He had married the white Desdemona. His friend Iago made him believe that his wife was not faithful to him. Othello being a very honest man never for a moment thought that other people were not, and believed Iago. Therefore he killed Desdemona, and then committed suicide after he found out she had always been faithful to him. I was not surprise that Desdemona loved Othello as hands as he was.

At least the actor who played him was. I wrote down notes about performances of the actors.

After the play I really wanted to meet the actors, who had done a splendid job with very good performances. I got Louise to come with me backstage. I first met the woman, who played Desdemona, and she introduced me to the director. It was very nice to meet them. I talked to the one, who played Iago. He was in reality married to the one, who played his wife, Emelie in the play. I was scared I would miss the lead actor, who played Othello, but he finally came, and was the last one we met. His name was Terence (not his real name), and I will call him Terry. He was very handsome with a moustache, and of course dark skinned like the Moor he was playing. He must have been interested in talking to me since he asked me for a cup of coffee in a restaurant, so I asked Louise if this would be all right. He drove us in the car I described above to a coffeehouse in the neighbourhood. Since I don´t drink coffee I had a Coca Cola. It was very interesting to talk to Terry. He is very intelligent and did not show any sign of being superior to us. This was as a matter of fact the first time he had played a leading role and did it so well. He was a teacher, and was doing further studies at the college. I got his autograph written on my program, and when we said good bye I thought I would never see him again.

I wrote my critic and read it for my drama class. I was a bit overwhelmed by having met all these actors. The next few days my mind was totally occupied thinking about Terry. I decided to write him a letter and sent him a photo of me, and asked him to correspond with me. It was not just that I thought that one day he might be a famous Hollywood actor. No, something unexplainable had happened to me. He had a terrific effect upon me.

Life went on, and I participated in an AFS day in Millikan High. There were pancakes for breakfast and entertainment. We visited a few classes and made speeches about our countries twice in a big auditorium. After that we went to The Tucker School which is for paralyzed and handicapped children. I found it very interesting to talk to them.

Same evening I went to a dance at the Elks Club with Ken Ludmerer. Ken is a Jew and I had never known people of that religion. There were three bands playing and we danced and had a good time. Count Basie had one of these bands. I got his autograph. After the dance we went to a restaurant, and I got a Coke float. This was chocolate ice cream put into the Coke, and then it became frothed. I had never tried nor heard of this before. I thought this was really very American. I often made this later on. Next day I went with my family to Santa Ana and Anaheim shopping. There I got something, also very American, called cool out which is pants, but looks like you are wearing a skirt. It has also been called a pants skirt. One had to wear a special petticoat pants with this. I got them also later with laces and frills. This was interesting.

There was going to be a play at my school, and it was called ´I Remember Mama'. It is about a Norwegian family in San Francisco. I was lucky enough to participate by getting a small part. Otherwise the actors were only the ones who had been studying drama the last couple of years. All the leading roles were cast by two to be able to give more students opportunities, and they took turns in playing. Ginnie Wright and Jill Taft played Kathrin. Mama was played by Pam Leonard and Darlene Walker. Bill Ohlman and Ralph Dougherty took turns in playing Nels and Uncle Chris. Jim Baker and Allen Clark played Papa and Mr. Hyde. I, Sandra Selter and Ruthann Taylor played hotel guests. I was wearing a pink, long dress, and had a blue hat, and a blue cape. We also had make up on. We had to practice a lot, and I was really excited to participate in this. After the last performance we were all invited to a party at the home of Jim Baker.

Since I had met Terry I started noticing more my fellow students, who were black. One day I was looking directly at a boy named Earl McCullough, who was a very good athlete, and our eyes met. I looked away as soon as he looked at me. I am not sure whether he knew who I was. This was embarrassing to be spotted looking at a boy. I even made friends with a black girl, called Saundra Grimmitt. We often spent our lunch break together. I told her about Terry, and she was excited. I waited and waited for my letter to him to be returned, because I was not sure I had sent it to the right place. I read a book called 'Black like me' by a white author, John Howard Griffin, who had his skin coloured to be able to have real experience of how it was to be a black person in the deep south of the United States. This was a very interesting story. It was also filmed. I have never been able to understand why people have to suffer for being dark skinned, and not having the same rights as whites. Not only that, but also had to suffer all sorts of humiliations for hundreds of years.

I sank into trying to understand this, and also read the book 'From the Back of the Bus' by Dick Gregory. He was a black entertainer and an entrepreneur. He used to get 10 dollars working as a car washer, but got 5 thousand dollars a week for telling about all of the injustice in his country. He always pointed out the funny side of things. This book was full of funny stuff in different situations. The titles points to the fact that in the south black people were only supposed to,and allowed to sit at the back of buses. Until one day a lady by the name of Rosa Parks refused to go to the back and sat at the front. This created a lot of havoc, and she and the event became world famous. She became a leader in the civil rights movement. Blacks were not allowed to go the same restaurants or bars as whites, and so on. Dick also made fun of how great it was to be in Florida because he could go wherever he wanted there. All he had to do was to change his name into Ricardo, and people would think he was from Cuba. Prejudices no matter how they were, are never good and mostly because of ignorance and no will to know, nor understand people of different origins.

I did not realize what a great influence and a life changer Terry had been to me, until many years later. I would probably not have been able to get to know my husband, if I had not known him very well before. My mind was occupied with what had happened to the letter I sent to Terry. What should I do with it if I got it back? Should I just keep it and open in a few years time? Perhaps I should try to call him and tell him about the letter? I had recently had a letter from an American man, Owen Goodman who was in the American armed forces, and was situated in Iceland. He wanted to correspond with me. He had got my name and address from relatives of the Webb family in California. He was bit bored in Iceland, so I thought it would be all right to be his pen pal. Apart from writing letters to family and friends in Iceland, I also had a pen pal in Sweden, who was a girl a bit younger than I.

One day I got a letter from a school and I thought it must be from one more Junior High school that wanted me to come and talk about Iceland. I saw on the stamp from which town it came from and was quick to open it. "My dearest Harpa" it started and it was from Terry! I was over the moon. He wanted to see me again, and go to a restaurant for coffee. I was to write to him again and decide when and what time. I thought he was perhaps testing me to see whether I meant what I had said in the letter. This was exciting. Another letter came this day telling me that my father had been ill and was in a hospital. I ran out to buy a get well Card for him. Then I replied to the letter from Terry, and waited in suspense for the answer.

I had to go and make a speech for mothers who had twins. As usual I was wearing my costume and everything went well. I met an Icelandic girl there called Loa and I went with her to a party for Icelanders. There were only Icelandic ladies there, and after such a long time emphasizing on speaking English every day, I had difficulties in speaking Icelandic. I would never have expected this.

We were invited to a trip on a warship. I could not sleep much during the night and kept on waking up. I was afraid I would not wake up with the alarm clock, because we had to be on time, and Marge was predicting I would not wake up. I got up at six thirty in the morning and went with the AFS kids and a boy called Dan Upton. He was a shipmate on the ship Oklahoma City. This was a very big warship and we sailed to Catalina Island near the coast of California. We sailed along the shores of the island but did not land there, nor get off the ship. Dan showed us all kinds of things on the ship. There were many other guests besides us so there were many shows going on. The weather was very good and the ship hardly moved on the still waters. It was good for me because I am usually very seasick. I did not feel any such thing now. It was an amazing experience to get to sail with this ship in the fresh sea air. It was an interesting and memorable day

17

Terry

Guess what?

Terry called me and I recognized his voice immediately. He spoke with a bit of an accent even though it was not as typical as many black people spoke.

He said first "Is this Harpa? Do you know who I am?"

I replied "yes, I think I know who you are. Who are you?"

He: "Guess. You don´t know."

I: "Yes, but tell me anyway."

He said "Terence."

He asked me if I was nervous, and I must have been and he felt it. He told me that he was twenty seven years old, and married to a girl of Scandinavian origin. He was supposed to play soon in another play that he would get paid for acting in. I had not given him my telephone number. So how could he be calling me? He had a friend who was working for a telephone company, and he found out my number for him. I was really impressed that he had gone to this trouble to be able to talk to me. We decided he would come to my home the following Saturday. He was going to call on the Wednesday before to arrange everything.

After this conversation I went out with Frank shopping. He bought a record for Marge for her birthday. It was their fifteenth birthday. I bought a baseball bat for him and a pearl necklace for Marge and a face powder.

As soon as we returned Terry called again saying he would not be able to come on Saturday, because he would be busy both rehearsing and signing papers for that new play. Instead he would pick me up from school after the weekend.

Would he actually come I wondered. He did. I waited on the curb and he came driving in that car, and I sat down inside. We drove down Atlantic Avenue. He needed to do an errand at the college, and after that we drove to Belmont Shore, where we got some refreshments. We then sat in the car and talked and talked about anything we could think of. I was surprised how easy and fun it was to talk to him. He drove me home, and we sat for about an hour in front of the house talking, mostly about the civil rights movement. We decided to be always honest with each other, and he asked me to write him another letter. I did so the very same evening. I was a little bit nervous when I came inside, because I had been so long outside in the car. I was scared I would have to explain anything. But MOM said she had some Pepsi Cola, and asked me why I had not invited him inside!

In school I very often sat in the rows where the black girls were sitting in my physical education class, even though there was no other white girl sitting there. Once I was standing in a row in front of a shop at lunchtime. There were only black students there. A boy behind me started arguing to the one in front of me about a nickel .He put his hand out open to take the nickel and did not get it. I did not like to listen to them and thought that perhaps this guy just does not have the money to give to the other one. I knew I had a nickel in my purse so I took it up and gave to the boy and said "did you need a nickel"? I was not sure he would accept it, but he did and to my surprise he said "thank you darling". In those days the communications between black and white people were not so common.

I was ironing my clothes when Terry called exactly at the time he had said he would. He was going to come and pick me up and meet my family. MOM was in the garden when he arrived, and he met her there, and chatted with her for a while. They drank beer and I cut my finger opening the cans for them. I guess I was this nervous. Terry and I went for a drive to Compton and visited his friend who lived there. It was nice talking to them. I felt like I was at home talking to Icelandic people. We sat in the kitchen just like at home, and somehow I felt I belonged with these people. Terry has been teaching dancing and has a good voice. He was soon going to sing in a birthday party of a famous Hollywood actor. They put on a record with Ray Charles, and we danced one dance. It was on the agenda to go and see his wife, but we never got around to do that .I really wanted to see what she looked like. I think though that it would have been awkward. She might also have suspected something. On the way home Terry sang 'Danny Boy', 'Summer Time' and a few other songs for me. I took a photo of him in front of the car this day. He came inside for a short time and now he met DAD and Marge. He said he would call after two days, Tuesday evening.

Terry called instead on Monday. We talked and talked about all kind of things. It made me think that he could not wait until Tuesday to call. He called again on Wednesday, and we decided he would come for a visit that evening. He now met Frank, who told me later that he had forgotten that he was black, and that he had gotten a bit of a shock to see him. Terry saw a book by Shakespeare on a shelf and started to read aloud from it, and I could not help laughing. I was in no mood to listen to poetry at that moment. We went afterwards for a drive to Belmont Shore and then to downtown Long Beach. Terry talked about that I was not even holding his arm. I said: "Are you joking? " He: "Why not? ´´ I: " I have no right to do this". Back in the car I told him that I would not have done this anyway, because I did not behave like that towards men. We went to the beach and walked there, and listened to the sounds of the ocean. It was a little bit windy, so we went for shelter behind a little house. I said I did not have a clue about how he was able to be there with me. He said he wanted to hug me, and he did. He asked how heavy I was, and lifted me up, and gave me another hug. Then he kissed me a few times, but was never pushy like I often feel boys are. I had never kissed a boy apart from my boyfriend Jonas the summer before. I told him that in the past if boys wanted to kiss me I felt like vomiting. But this time I did not feel that way. However I never ever kissed him back. I just felt I did not have any right to do this because he was married. He said I did not know what kind of a relationship he had with his wife. He also said that there were many reasons for a marriage, when I asked why he had married her. I said I felt guilty about this, but he said I did not have to feel bad nor worry about it. Why did he want to do this? I wondered. What was more surprising was that I really liked it. I was glad that he felt this intimate with me. "We are just snooping around and hiding behind a house" I said when we walked to the car. "Well we are not there anymore" he said and lifted me up. He told me over and over again that I looked so good, and my hair was blowing in the breeze from the sea. He was also looking really good with those very white teeth. I really felt good and it was a wonderful evening. The sea looked turquoise and the moon was yellow. We had to take our shoes off, and empty the sand before entering the car. We went directly home. On the way he kissed me all of a sudden and said I would have to watch out when he had a gleam in his eye. I just laughed."Don´t you dare be romantic then" he said. "I´ll tell you one day how I feel" he said.

He was not going to come inside, but did anyway for a short time. He told me more about Othello and played a bit from the last act. He also read a few lines from a play called ´Sunny Morning.'

We continued being in touch on the phone, and he wrote me a love letter. He came and picked me up, and we went to the town where he was teaching, and to a park which was his favorite. It was so dark there that I could hardly see his face. It never even imagined that I could be in any kind of danger being there alone with him. I trusted him completely. As before, we chatted endlessly. I had written down seventeen things I wanted to discuss with him, and we managed to talk about most of them. I always thought anything he said was so wise. I worried about his wife, and that we were seeing each other. Still I could not think of anybody else. He also said he could not take his mind off me. On the way home he stopped the car and we were going to talk some more. A short while later we heard the noise of an ambulance and a police car came rushing. It stopped, and the policemen asked us if we had seen anything suspicious and how long we had been sitting there. A man had been found lying there very close by. He had been stabbed. We were lucky not to be involved in any trouble because of this. We had been too occupied with each other to notice anything.

"If you continue to look at me this way I am going to kiss you." Terry said before I went inside my home. I guess I could not hide how much I admired him. I really truly wished that he had not been married. I always had a guilty feeling seeing him, and did not feel that I had any right to do this.

One day I had to wait until four in the afternoon for him to pick me up after school. I was with my friend Saundra who was both pretty and fun.

When he came we went to a shop that sold tea shirts and sweaters with all kinds of slogans. He was thinking to start a business with a very special slogan regarding the civil rights movement. Afterwards we went to a restaurant where I got a milkshake. All of a sudden three of my school sisters appeared there. I have no idea what they thought when they saw us there together. Nobody ever mentioned it to me. Once more we went to Belmont shore.

We continued our friendship. Terry called and sent me a letter where he said we would have to let fate lend a hand and so on. One evening we went to San Pedro where he showed me a place called ´The Light House ´where jazz was played. We could not enter because I was only eighteen and you had to be twenty one to enter. He really liked jazz. I did not know much about that kind of music. That day my family, DAD, MOM, Marge and Frank had left for a trip to Europe, and I was alone at home apart from

Grandma, who was in her little house in the garden. I asked Terry to come inside. He picked me up and carried me up the stairs.

I showed him some things in my room. He kissed me and kissed me, and said he wanted to be close to me. He said he loved me and wanted to make love to me."I love you, you know that" he said "you are much more of a woman than I thought you were". He always smelled so nice. It must have been a fragrance of some cologne he used. I have never come across any man with the same smell. We were lying fully clothed on my bed and he was a bit nervous. He never tried to do make any advances nor touch me in sensitive places. I did not encourage him in any way either. I knew he wanted me because I was so near to him that I could feel the bulge in his trousers. I was cool.

I was happy, and wished he could stay the whole night, but I knew he would have to go home. I was certainly not going to do anything stupid, and I was not going to lose my virginity with a man I could not have any future with. I was definitely in love with him. He thought I was doing him a favour by letting him kiss me, even though I did not kiss him back. I never told him that I loved him. I never told a single soul about what happened that night.

I had a farewell party for my friends and had also invited Saundra, but she did not come. She wrote me a letter where she told me she had to go to a church event. We corresponded for some time. I thought perhaps she did not dare to come to an all white party. It was not regular that black kids were hanging around with white kids. I also invited Terry and he came, and was very good looking. He chatted with Reed and Mary Ann, who had moved in, and chaperoned while the family was away. Terry offered to drive me to Culver City, where my trip across the US was going to start in a few days, but Reed and Mary Ann said they would do it. I played some records, and Terry and I danced before he left. He kissed me a light kiss at the door, the last kiss. I never saw him again.

My school brothers and sisters were happy with all the snacks and other things I had bought for them. After they had all gone I played the song where it says 'It´s my party and I cry if I want to', because I was near to crying myself after saying bye to Terry and I also played 'Sealed with a kiss'.

The next morning Terry called me to say a proper good bye, but we did not talk for a long time. He said it was too difficult for him and I felt the same. I cried and cried afterwards. The thought that we would never ever see each other again was unbearable. Up to now this has been my secret.

18

The End Was Near

The time passed very quickly and before I knew it was spring and it was starting to get warmer. Sometimes it was about 80F (25C) which was very comfortable. Marge and I sometimes went onto the roof and were sunbathing there. I always had plenty to do especially socially. I have always been very sociable and enjoyed participating in all those events. One of my school sisters Marcia Merritt was dancing the lead of Swanhilda in a ballet called Coppelia I went to see this and Marcia was a great ballerina.

I was so unlucky to break one of my fingers on my right hand playing volleyball. Not very comfortable. I was taken to a doctor and an x-ray was taken. I had to have a piece made of metal under the finger for support for the next 6 weeks. It was difficult to write anything so I had to try to use my left hand for that.

MOM invited me to Marineland. It was a new experience for me and nice to see the whales and how the sea lions performed their tricks. She gave me a broach for memory of this place.

I went to a saloon and had my hair cut. Had not done this before in this country. It was very expensive for me and cost twenty five dollars with a tip. This tip business was a total mystery to me. Also when I wanted to buy something, and came to a counter to pay it was always more because some taxes were added. I found this rather ridiculous. When my school sisters saw me with the short hair they thought that I had colored my hair. I had not. I am a brunette, and my hair had gotten so much lighter during the many months in the sun.

Everyone was excited about the events coming up. The All Night Dance which was called that because it did not start until about 11 in the evening and lasted until the middle of the night and The Prom which was the main dance of the year. I went with my friend Robert (Bob) Bormann to both these events. We had been hanging around at school together for some time. He wanted to wear my necklace, and he gave me also something to wear. Then people started asking if we were going steady. I said no straight away. I was not even interested in him. You can say that he admired me. I did not really know much about how he felt otherwise. He wrote a few nice poems for me and gave me. I wore the same pink dress to the Prom that I had worn at the PHI GAMMA CHI Christmas dance. I didn´t have a fancy dress like some of the other girls were wearing. MOM had given me nice white satin shoes to wear. The boys were also wearing nice suits or tuxedos. I did not enjoy being with Bob at these dances. My mind was totally with somebody else.

Preparations for graduation from the school were going on and we had to practice walking in rows in a big auditorium downtown. There were two different ceremonies. They were at the Long Beach Arena the very place Miss Iceland had won the beauty pageant, Miss International the year before. The graduation ceremony was very solemn and we had to walk very slowly. The music was playing and the main one was a part of Ludwig van Beethoven´s ninth symphony. We were wearing grey gowns and with a cap on our heads. Some speeches were made, and we got our High School Diploma. Here it was a great achievement for young people. I have never needed this diploma since I had already fulfilled all qualifications for college. I had also taken some special examinations in Iceland before. Our yearbook Caeruela had been published. It was a nice book with lots of photos and articles about everything that had happened during the school year. There were pictures of the athletes, the homecoming queen, the princesses, the Song girls, Flag girls, Polyettes, the cheerleaders members of all the clubs, the choirs, the bands and so on. There was a photo of me and Suphan on the AFS page. I was also in photos in three other places in the book. The last few days in the school we had our books handy and were busy writing messages in them. Many wrote very nice things and said they were happy to have gotten to know me and would miss me. We sometimes only signed our name on the page where the photo of the friend was. There were pictures of all the teachers and other workers. There was a picture of each and every one of the students starting with the juniors and ending with us graduates. The names were under the photos with the last name first.

I will always be grateful for everything my families did for me and the opportunities I got. They were the Janich family and the Webb family in Long Beach California. This was the most fantastic year of my life.

19

The Trip Across The United States

California, Arizona, New Mexico, Texas.

I was so lucky to be in California and therefore got the opportunity to travel with a bus across the United States for a few weeks with forty three exchange students from many countries. Some of the students I had met before at meetings, but most of them, I had never seen before. Our trip started in Culver City with a swimming pool party. I was hosted by the Tarn family. There were four children Bill, Bob, Tom and a daughter I never saw. I got her room and slept in her bed sheets. They had not changed them. I did not say anything. In the evening there was a picnic and after that Bill took me to a folk song party. Songs like 'I´m 500 miles from home', 'Kumbaya', 'Blowing in the Wind 'and 'Where have all the flowers gone' were among the songs. I learned these songs and they were also amongst many other songs we sang on the bus. After the party we went to a drive in restaurant and ordered food. At this time there was no such restaurant in Iceland. I was endlessly experiencing new things.

The next morning we had an orientation meeting about our trip, and how we should behave. The exchange students were from twenty nine countries, among them Norway, Denmark, Sweden, Germany, Spain, Portugal, India and Peru. I was the only one from Iceland. Aruna from India who had been in a Wilson High was also there. This was a bunch of happy teenagers, who were looking forward to the trip. We all had just said our goodbyes to our families and friends and there was a certain sorrow also. Now we had to emphasize on getting to know each other the best we could. We got to visit Culver City High School where the meeting was being held.

After lunch we went to see the Metro-Golden-Mayer film studios, which was in this city. We saw a big area where walls were painted for outside scenes, and looking like the sky and the sea. We saw a replica of the ship that was used in the movie 'Mutiny on the Bounty'. It was half burned. There were streets there full of houses where you could only see the front. It was all a fake. Then there were all sorts of trees, ships and canals. I found this all very fascinating.

In the evening there was a party at the school. Records were played, and we danced. Bill came with me there. When we arrived home he wanted to kiss me a good night kiss. I said "No, thank you, I am not for that kind of things". I was not interested in him, nor anybody else. I could not forget Terry. I was in a deep sorrow. Just as good that Bill did not know who got to kiss me before!

The family and I got along very well and I corresponded with the mother for the next ten years. I have not been able to find out what happened to them after that. Our big trip started the next morning. A long linen banner was stretched along one side of the bus. We had decorated it and written our names on it. People were really going to see that exchange students were on the go. Our bus was number eleven and we said it was ´fantafic´ made up of two words (fantastic+terrific). So we had made up a new word. Of course we had guides with us, a young woman called Gerri Logan and a young man called John Burmahln. They were both university students. They were to take care of us the next three weeks. It was decided to write a diary about this trip and we took turns in writing. I always wrote a diary anyway, so it was not big deal for me. Only thing that bothered me was that I had to use my left hand to write because of my broken finger.

We headed first to Chandler, Arizona. On the way we stopped in Indio for a lunch break. It was terribly hot. It was like stepping into an oven coming out of the bus. It was difficult to sit on the bus in over a hundred degrees Fahrenheit, because the air condition had broken down in this Continental Trail Ways bus. Some of the kids smoked, and were allowed to do this at the back of the bus. We had to hurry to eat any fruit we had from California, because it was forbidden to take any fruits across the state line. We saw to Greyhound buses on the way that had broken down. We thought that perhaps some other AFS students were there but it did not turn out to be so. Later we actually met with lots of them who were on bus number twelve. They had a punctured tire and were delayed. So were we.

In Chandler I stayed with the Tyler family. There was a girl called Susan and a boy called Jim. Susan who was twelve years old was interested in corresponding with my sister Inga who was eleven. Next day we went into the countryside and looked at airplanes because the father was a pilot. Then we went and saw a potato factory where lots of Mexicans were working. The potatoes were washed and were on a conveyor belt and were coloured red. I found that very strange. Perhaps they owners thought they would be looking more appealing. They were then to be taken by train to the markets. After this we visited a farm where cotton was grown. This is very commonly grown in Arizona. A house was being built from special new bricks and I found that modern. I wrote about this in our diary on Bus eleven.

After a busy day it was refreshing in the heat to swim in the family swimming pool. The lady of the house had graduated from Poly High just like me and showed me her yearbooks. We were all invited for dinner to the family who hosted Wolf from Germany and Gina from Costa Rica. We discussed a lot of things like the maturity of American teenagers and the racism problem. We talked about that people were created equal as was in the constitution of the US. Why, were all people not treated equal?

"Would you allow your sister to marry a black man?" This was a good question, because a lot of people thought they did not have anything against blacks, but just did not want to be a part of their family. They did not think of themselves as racists.

After bidding farewells to our host families we sang our bus song and shouted out a triple hurrey for them the next morning. Then we were on our way to Carlsbad, New Mexico. We had a meeting in the bus and formed many committees. Some had the task to take the suitcases off the bus, and also to load them on to the bus. We elected Wolf from Germany and Julie from Greece to be the entertainment guys and Akira from Japan was the president.

We stopped in Tucson for a bit. Then there was an endless desert and a lot of heat on the way. We were very glad to reach Lordsburg and have some refreshments and ate our pack lunches. We had a meeting discussing our entertainment in the spirit of AFS. Siew Beh from Malayshia divided us into six groups that were Asia, Central Europe, Scandinavia, southern Europe, South America and the countries belonging to the United Kingdom. A chairman was chosen for each area. On the way to El Paso, Texas we were singing a lot of songs and also started practicing some of the entertainments. We thought it kind of weird that we could have jumped over to Mexico from El Paso. Finally we reached Carlsbad, and with a police escort! I stayed with the Abernathy family. The couple had four children Perry twenty years old, Janet was eighteen, Holly thirteen and Beth five. Gerri and John also stayed there.

Very early next morning we went to see the Carlsbad caves which are about an hour drive from the city. Indians had discovered these caves a long time ago but in the year 1898 a teenager by the name of Jim White climbed down into the caves with a homemade wire ladder. He named all the different chambers. These caves are very large. We walked inside and were there for about three and a half hours. There were huge lime stones hanging from the ceilings. They had been created for millions of years. It was totally amazing. At the end we came into a large visitor center, where we could sit down and have our lunch. It was rather cold down there. It was interesting that after all this walk we did not have to go back, nor climb out somewhere else because we could take an elevator up. This was about six stories to get to the surface.

In the evening we were able to participate in different sports in the local school. I found this a bit boring and wondered into another area. There was a beauty contest there and Miss Carlsbad was elected. I did not know her name.

The weather was very nice and a beautiful sunshine. We spent the next day by the river and swam in it. There were all sorts of boats and a jumping board. We sailed on a boat, and for the first time I tried water skiing. I was not good at this at all, and kept on falling into the river. Besides that my swimming costume was not good for this. The way the force of the water made it almost fall off, and my broken finger got all wet. I still had something on the finger for protection, and a splinter. I just stopped this experiment. I really think it must be lot of fun to do this, if one can stand properly on the skis. I got some sunburn after being there for hours.

When we got back to the house we went horseback riding. I was wearing my new and nice cowboy hat that the Tyler family in Chandler had given me as a souvenir. Many people wore them in this area. I had not been on a horseback for a long time and thought it was a bit of a shake. Of course this horse was a whole lot larger than Icelandic horses. They are a little bit like ponies. I was shaking a lot, and once I went so much to one side, that I almost fell off.

After a barbeque dinner in the evening, all of us in Bus eleven had a show for our hosts and guests. We introduced our countries and sang and danced. I danced a Norwegian folk dance along with the kids from Denmark, Norway and Sweden. I had not danced this dance before, and once I made a mistake. I laughed so hard that I could hardly continue, but of course I had to. John had a movie camera and he took movies of all of this. After our show American boys came wearing Indian costumes (native) and danced Indian dances. They were very good. I think everyone had a good time.

I had been composing a letter to Terry in my mind and wrote it that evening.

Next we went to the biggest state Texas, where the inhabitants want to show what is the biggest, best or only available in their state. We drove through Dallas, where the horrible murder of Kennedy took place last twenty second of November. We stayed in a town near by the city called Fort Worth. Television people were waiting for us when we arrived there, and news about us coming to town was on the evening news. Some students were interviewed by journalists, but I was not. Articles and pictures were in the newspapers the next day.

I stayed with the Stuck couple who had Susan and two other daughters who were not at home. We were now in the south, where many white people did not want to have anything to do with black people. Two black maids worked for this family, and each of them came every other day to work. They were good enough to clean! The family said a prayer before the meals. I had only seen this in films. Eating a delicious sweet melon for breakfast was new to me.

We went to the amusement park Six Flags which is their Disneyland. It was really fun to be there. After that we went for a picnic at the YMCA, and again we entertained with song and dance. A television crew took some films.

Oklahoma, Kansas, Missouri, Illinois and Indiana.

Off we went again with Bus eleven on the national roads. Next stop was Oklahoma city and I stayed there with the Wyler family and the daughter there was Claudia. On our way to a party in the evening, Claudia was driving a Thunderbird car. She was so unlucky to drive on a chain that was stretched across the road. She did not see it because it was so dark. The car got smashed on the side where I was sitting, because she had hit a pillar. I got lots of mud all over me and my eye hurt after hitting something when the car had been shaking. Otherwise we were both all right, and went right ahead to the party. The host Mr. Furmann collected Icelandic stamps, and had a friend who had been in Iceland, and written a book about Icelandic birds. I found this remarkable. He was going to send me some stamps. I got this book autographed by the author as a present.

When the family found out that I had never traveled with a train, they decided to invite me on a trip on a train. Claudia and I were driven the next morning to Guthrie and boarded a train. I thought this was very exciting and looked at many of the carriages. We had breakfast on board the train. Most of the workers there were coloured. We took the train to a town called Norman, and the couple waited for us there when we arrived. Then we drove through the University campus in Oklahoma. After that I bought a record with a group called The Lettermen, which was sung by a very popular group of young men. I also bought a record with Mario Lanza, who I admired very much.

Claudia and I went to a fun park called Frontier City, which was a lot like Knottsberry Farm in California. A farm in the southern states was staged. Slaves were shown working on the farm. And everything about their life in the olden days was shown. This was very interesting and well done.

One more picnic in the evening and our entertainment.

We drove from Oklahoma through the state of Kansas with a short stop in Wichita, and through Kansas City to a small town called Grain Valley, Missouri near there. During the night there were thunders and lightings. The Independence Day, fourth of July had arrived, the national holiday of the United States. It was disappointing not to see any celebrations of any kind. We could not see any signs of that anything special was happening. Still there was a protest march against the situation of black people. One of the AFS students, a boy from Italy was warned that perhaps he would not be permitted into a restaurant. The reason: Yes, he had become so tan in the sunshine! Of course people were just joking about this.

I stayed with the Norris family and so did Birgit from Germany. Most of the families in this town were hosting three to four students. In this home were three daughters Jane twelve years old, Terry fifteen and Nancy eighteen. As AFS practices:"Where there is a room in the heart, there is a place to stay." It was very true here.

We went to see Fort Osage, which was an old fort. We also swam in the family pool when we felt like it. Small children cracked some Chinese crackers in the evening, but we were forbidden to do anything like that. Some had bought some stuff like that and were very disappointed not being able to celebrate this national holiday. Kids from bus twelve were there with us in the evening, and there was a talent competition between us and them. We did very well, and were more organized, but the other group may have been more talented. We also competed in soccer and bus twelve won us. We felt we had won in spirit though because we cheered our team by shouting a lot. Later we had discussions about different matters, religion, politics, boys and girls and morality etc.

We said good bye to Grain Valley in the warmth of summer and headed further east. Of course we looked at the landscape on the way through the windows. There was always fun and we sang the songs I had mention before and also songs like 'Oh, my darling Clementine', 'Swing Low, Swing Chariot', 'I´ve been working on the railroad', 'Tom Dooley' 'Jamaica Farewell' (better known as Kingston Town), 'This land is your land', 'Mariah', 'He´s got the whole world in his hands' and 'When the saints come marching in'. In the last song we changed it to 'When AFS comes marching in' and thought that was appropriate.

We arrived in St. Louis around noon and met up with a lot of AFSers who had been traveling in four buses. We were thrilled to meet some of the students who had been with us during the year. I noticed how many black people were in this city. We continued right across Illinois to Indiana and there was pouring rain on the way. Next stop Colombus, Indiana and it kept on raining plus thunders and lightings.

I was now with the Edwards family Debbie and Mark. We were all tired after the trip and rested the next morning. In the afternoon I went shopping with Yuko Hashimoto from Japan. As a whole I found this a very boring day. I was also restless, because I had not heard anything from Terry. Even though we were travelling we could receive mail. I was not sure whether he knew this. Still I was waiting for a reply. It did not come until I had gone back home.

In the evening we had hamburgers in Lincoln Center and we put on our show. After that we were told that we were supposed to dance with Americans. I asked some of them, and they just did not want to dance. I was not used to that a girl should ask a boy to dance and was very upset. I thought this was humiliating. Perhaps they just did not know how to dance at all. Yoko and I left and went back to the house and watched TV. Then I finished writing a letter to Owen Goodman.

Ohio, Pennsylvania, New York.

Next morning we found out that some of the kids had been far too long time in the party the night before. The hosts did not even know where they were. This was very serious and rules broken. We always had to follow the rules and be role models in honour of our nations. In no way could we break any rules. We left for another Columbus, now the one in Ohio and had lunch there. Columbus is a very popular name for towns and they are named after Christopher Columbus, who they believe discovered America. I say believe, because we always correct this by telling them about Leifur Eiriksson, who was there long before in the year one thousand. He called the land Vineland, because there were vineyards there. The United States gave Iceland a nice statue of Leifur. It is situated in front of the Hallgrimskirkja (a church) on top of a hill overlooking Reykjavik.

On the way to Leechburg our bus broke down. The breaks were not working properly. We had to stop in a town called Steubenville. We all had to leave the bus while it was being repaired. We wondered around and some of us did some shopping and the bus driver paid for everything. I and two other kids bought ice cream and got all messy on the fingers. This was in a black area and we talked to a few of people. One woman invited us in to wash our hands. We were glad to be able to do that. Once inside we saw a total mess and I had never, ever seen anything like it. Everything was also very dirty. She said she was both cleaning and painting at the same time. But it was very nice of her to invite us inside.

We went all to a restaurant where I met a man called Tom Davis. He had been stationed in the armed forces in Iceland. We got free chewing cum and a journalist came to interview us and a photographer took photos of us. This was new that exchange students came all of a sudden to this town. We were also invited to a cinema to watch the film ´What a way to go´ with Shirley MacLain, Dean Martin and Dick van Dyke. This was fun. We were overjoyed about how nice the people of Steubenville were to us. It took a long time to repair the bus so we could not leave until eleven thirty in the evening.

We stopped in Pittsburg for an hour and then I met Anna Ingolfsdottir, who had come with me on the plain from New York to Los Angeles last summer. She had been staying in Chino, California, and was also on her bus trip. The people in Leechburg had been waiting for us, and were happy to see us. They stood with placards welcoming us.

We usually only stayed two nights in every city so we were packing, and coming, and going all the time. I guess I am a gypsy by heart, because it suited me just fine. We kept on meeting new and new people. Everywhere the people were nice and hospitable .They always wanted to show us as much as possible of their place or the area near .Most of these people I have never, ever seen again. We sent thank you letters to all of them after each visit. I bought postcards from each and every state and city we visited. I also bought many souvenirs. This all had to be small because we had only been allowed to carry one suitcase and a hand luggage. A few weeks before the trip I had sent one suitcase back home with clothes and other things.

The family I stayed wit in Leechburg was the Nigro family. The couple had three children youngest Jeffrey three, Lisa five and Kathy nine years old. A chicken was bought at a restaurant, and then we took it with us for a picnic in the evening. After that there was a party behind the local church. Next day a few of us went to Pittsburg and were roaming around there. I really liked to be in the big city. Nat KIng Cole was entertaining that evening, but we could not see him because we had to put on our show as usual. I was wearing my costume and Aruna and Latika from India were wearing their saris. I changed my clothes before the dance started. It was a lot of fun. By this time some of the students on our bus had become very close and there were a few pairs. Most of us were good friends and had known each other for those weeks. I talked less with others. I only thought about Terry, and had no interest in getting to know the boys closely.

There was no chance that I would get some boyfriend on the bus.

Our next stop was a bit longer in White Plains, New York. The Svibruck family welcomed me and there were Cathy fifteen, Ted also fifteen and Jon sixteen years old. The boys had been adopted. One day I went with the mother and Cathy to visit a black family that lived in Long Island. This was the Cannon family where Pricilla was the eldest fifteen, Allan eight and Ellen five years old. The children were very cute, and very nice with me. I played Matador with Allan, and chatted with their parents. We brought a cake for them.

We went to New York the next day and visited Rockefeller Center. There was a guide who talked like a robot. I did not like that, nor what we saw. We went up to the seventieth story, which was the highest. Too much fog hindered our views. Because of this I got a ticket permitting me to return, and it was valid until the next century! We stopped by at The Loftleidir Icelandic office, but did not find any Icelanders there. After lunch we took three subway trains to where we could go with the ferry to Staten Island to see the Statue of Liberty. It was still some fog and not as interesting. We took an elevator to a platform and climbed from there to the crown. Later this was not permitted, to preserve the statue. I took some photos as I had been doing the whole time. Back again on the train to Greenwich Village, the artists area. We did not see much there though. Now it was pouring rain and we became soaking wet walking from a bus to a restaurant. Next we went with a bus to Chinatown. Cathy´s father had a shop there. We roamed around and saw the Chinese shops and restaurants. We saw Latika from India, Gisele from The Netherlands and Shinpei from Japan, all friends from Bus eleven. They were also sightseeing in the big city.

We had planned to go and see Othello in an outdoor theater. James Earl Jones played the leading role. It would have been nice to compare Terry´s performance to the famous professional actor. I could never do that. The performance was cancelled due to the rain. We took a taxi to the railway station, which was situated right next door to The Commodore Hotel in 42nd street where I had stayed last summer.

The World´s Fair was held this summer in New York and also in 1965. We went to see it. It was a huge area with all kinds of buildings. Different countries from round the world had them built and introduced their culture, new technology and their produces. A big replica of the earth had been made of metal. We were not able to see everything but looked at the buildings where Switzerland, Denmark, Spain, Africa, Coca Cola and Du Pont were representing their things. In the last one people could talk to people i films. In the African one the there were dancers wearing hardly anything. They had small pieces of leather material on. I met a boy from Kenya and another one from Liberia whose name was Francois

Massaquai. He seemed to be very clever and decisive. He was studying politics at a university. He aimed for being a president in Liberia. We became pen friends, and he wanted to come to Iceland. That never happened, and I did not become the first lady, as he wanted at one time. I think he later became a sports minister in Liberia. Some years ago I got an email from somebody with the same last name, and from the same country. I thought perhaps he was my friend´s son, but never found out.

Debbie Reynolds the famous film actress came there riding in a carriage. I ran and took a nice photo of her, and also got her autograph. Mr. Stephen Galatti the president of AFS had died the day before. All the AFS students who were at the World Fair this day, showed their respect with a one minutes silence in the memory of a remarkable man. He was seventy five years old and had been the president for twenty nine years. He was very well respected. We were about one hundred and fifty people who stood there around the globe. The students in Bus eleven dedicated our diary of our trip across the United States to him, in his honour.

The last night in White Plains we gave our guides presents after our usual show. John and Gerry had done such a good job. I thought John was the major guide. We became penpals for many years, and he sent me many pictures from Malaysia, where he went to work for the Peace Corps. When he had finished this mission he came and visited me in Iceland. We got to see the film he had been taking of our show. Everyone was a bit sad both because of the death of Mir. Galatti and also because we knew that soon our trip would be over and it would be very difficult to depart with our travel companions. Most of us said "if you come to my country you have to visit me". The enthusiasm and interest was great. I don´t know how many of them visited each other in the next years to come. I only met Gunter from Germany a few years later in Berlin. Our last trip with Bus eleven was from White Plains to Washington D.C. We said our good byes in case we would not be able to see each other in the capital. Many cried. Everybody had got their nickname. I was named ´Miss Precise´. Sometimes people think I am too accurate. I just did not realize that they had also noticed.

Washington D.C and Virginia.

We were driven to a big army airport and the lots of buses started arriving there. We met a lot of people we knew. I met all the Icelanders, most of them I had not seen since August last year. We stopped there for awhile and could compare notes about our experiences during our time in the States. Then we went to new buses. Gudmundur Karlsson from Iceland was there. Next to me sat a boy from Ethiopia. His name was Nur Reja. He started flirting with my right away.

I stayed with the Paige family in Alexandria in Western Virginia. Liz Kupp, a guide also stayed there, and Yildrim from Turkey. Cynthia fourteen years old and her brother Roger eighteen years old lived here. Cynthia and I became friends and penpals and kept up the friendship up to now, even though she moved later between states, married, divorced, remarried, and became a widow. We did not get a chance to see each other until forty five years later.

There was a meeting early next morning. Most of the time I sat next to Nur, but he was very pushy just like Icelandic boys, I thought. I did not think he was cute, but still wanted to be somewhere near him these days. I think it was only important to him that I was a girl. I don´t think he really liked me very much. I didn´t want to have anything to do with him in the way he wanted. The main reasons I wanted to be near him was to show everybody that I was not a racist. Sometimes we would hold hands and as I said before it was not common for a white girl and a black boy to be seen together in public. One Indian had also wanted to hold hands with me. Perhaps this was a practise for me, so I would be able to walk hand in hand with my future husband just a year later in the main street of Reykjavik? Sometimes it is like everything in life is destined.

In the evening we went to a concert held by the Watergate. An orchestra played on a floating stage on the Potomac River. Among other songs they played ´When the Saints come marching in´ and the AFS students sang loudly '' When AFS comes marching in '' along. This was a lot of fun, and everyone was in good spirits. This was near the Lincoln Memorial so we went there also. A big statue Abraham Lincoln one of the presidents of the United States is situated there. He sits in a big armchair in front of a big white building, Roman style. He was most famous for fighting for stopping the slavery of black men in the south. The Southerners were not happy about this. They wanted to have free labors to pick cotton and work on the big plantations. Civil war between the south and the north had been going on, and still there were some problems between these parts of the country. President Lincoln was shot in the Ford Theater on April 14th 1865 by an actor called John Wilkes Booths. He did so because he believed Abraham was a really bad person. The president was moved across the street to a house called Peterson House and was in coma until the next day when he died. Before, he had been getting many death threats for a long time from different persons.

We had more meetings and then went to The Mall and looked at that. Then we visited the Smithsonian Museum, where I met Yuko from Japan and we spent a lot of time looking at all the interesting things at the museum. After that we went to the Washington memorial. There was such a big queue that we never got to go up inside it. This one is for the remembrance of the first president of the US George Washington. We ended by seeing the Capitol where the parliament resides.

Next day we went to Mt. Vernon and visited the home of George Washington the first president of The United States. After that we went to an Islamic Center which was for people believing in prophet Muhammed, now called islamists. We visited a beautiful mosque. There were carpets everywhere on the floors and people were praying. Afterwards we went to another religious place, the Cathedral of Washington, which was still under construction. I had a piece for a necklace made out of a coin with the church on it. In the evening there was one more party where we were dancing. I danced a lot with Nur and also with Ali from Iran. I was a bit miserable and decided to go outside. There was an area near with lots of trees, but no houses. I started walking and went further and further and did not see anybody. Then I thought this was not such a good idea. I could get lost or something might happen to me, so I returned to the house. I did not tell Nur that I wanted somehow to escape from this party.

The Icelandic exchange students were all invited for lunch at the Icelandic embassy by ambassador Thor Thors and his wife. A journalist came, and a photographer who took a photo of me and an American girl for a newspaper. A group photo was taken in front of the embassy, and that one appeared in the biggest newspaper in Iceland, called Morgunbladid. Oli Thoroddsen and I went for a walk and chatted. It came a pouring rain so we ran under a shelter at a bus stop. Then Oli said "this is not for a white man to be in this weather!" All around us were many black people. I could not help laughing. But this is a common sentence in Iceland when things are not going fine.

We had some refreshments on the bus and went on ahead to the White House. The weather had improved and was quite good when we were roaming around on the grass in front of the White House building. A brass band was playing and President Lyndon B. Johnsons appeared. We all stood up from our chairs. He held a small speech for us standing on a platform. When he stepped down, a lot of students gathered in front of him and shook his hand. I could have done the same but did not try hard enough. His wife Ladybird was there too and their daughters. It was John F. Kennedy I had been looking forward to see.

After that we went to a show at a place called The Armory where kids from around the world entertained. Nur sat with me in the bus and behaved the same. He had been with some Indian girl who was more cooperative than I, he said. He always complained that I was not. He was not happy and said that I was like a robot. He just needed to put a key inside and it would start. He was so angry with me that he changed the seat. I did not care. The next day he sat next to a Greek girl, and Jerry from Germany sat with me on the way from Washington to New York.

That morning was our very last meeting with the other AFS students. Robert Kennedy who was the minister of justice held a speech for us in a big arena. There was a huge response to his words and cheers just like the roof would fly off. We who had been together in Long Beach had a photo taken of us. I have not seen any of them again apart from Suphan which I met in New York thirty years later. He had returned to study at a university, and was a professor at a university there. He had married a Chinese girl and they had two children. They lived in Newark.

The last good bye took place and there were lots of hugs and kissing. Many cried, even the boys. I was with Nur, and also talked to some other boys from Ethiopia. I felt they were all flirting. In Long Island I said good bye to Nur and doubted he would ever write to me. I was wrong. He did write to me back home. The Icelandic students had to wait and wait to be transferred to a school in Westbury. I stayed with the Kraemer family and the children there were Gail seventeen years old, Dwight nineteen and Scott was ten.

We went shopping the next morning among the shops were the largest store in the United States Macy´s where I had also been the year before. I bought some stuff for my family back home. Then we went to the airport and the name of the airplane was called 'Snorri Þorfinnsson' after an Icelandic explorer. Some of the other AFS students from Europe had come to the US on the ship "Seven Seas" and had a lot of fun. They also returned to their home on the same ship.

I found it interesting to see the houses below looking like toys. We had some thunder weather on the way but everything went well. My parents and my sisters greeted me at the airport. The younger one was only five years old. She asked "who is this woman?" I must have changed a lot during my time away since she didn´t remember me at all.

I came back intact and not engaged to any man. On the other hand I probably got engaged to the whole black race and other dark skinned people for life.

THE EXCHANGE STUDENT   83

Printed in the United States
By Bookmasters